Tourism — Europe, Central European Countries, Mediterranean Countries

Key figures 1999–2000

EUROPEAN
COMMISSION

eurostat

THEME 4
Industry,
trade
and services

.... Immediate access to harmonised statistical data

Eurostat Data Shops:

A personalised data retrieval service

In order to provide the greatest possible number of people with access to high-quality statistical information, Eurostat has developed an extensive network of Data Shops (¹).

Data Shops provide a wide range of **tailor-made services**:

- ★ immediate information searches undertaken by a team of experts in European statistics;
- ★ rapid and personalised response that takes account of the specified search requirements and intended use;
- ★ a choice of data carrier depending on the type of information required.

Information can be requested by phone, mail, fax or e-mail.

(¹) See list of Eurostat Data Shops at the end of the publication.

Internet:

Essentials on Community statistical news

- ★ Euro indicators: more than 100 indicators on the euro-zone; harmonised, comparable and free of charge;
- ★ About Eurostat: what it does and how it works;
- ★ Products and databases: a detailed description of what Eurostat has to offer;
- ★ Indicators on the European Union: convergence criteria; euro yield curve and further main indicators on the European Union at your disposal;
- ★ Press releases: direct access to all Eurostat press releases.

For further information, visit us on the Internet at: www.europa.eu.int/comm/eurostat/

A great deal of additional information on the European Union is available on the Internet.
It can be accessed through the Europa server (http://europa.eu.int).

Cataloguing data can be found at the end of this publication.

Luxembourg: Office for Official Publications of the European Communities, 2001

ISBN 92-894-2058-8

EUROSTAT

L-2920 Luxembourg — Tel. (352) 43 01-1 — Telex COMEUR LU 3423
Rue de la Loi 200, B-1049 Bruxelles — Tel. (32-2) 299 11 11

Eurostat is the Statistical Office of the European Communities. Its task is to provide the European Union with statistics at a European level, that allow comparisons to be made between countries and regions. Eurostat consolidates and harmonizes the data collected by the Member States.

To ensure that the vast quantity of accessible data is made widely available, and to help each user make proper use of the information, Eurostat has set up a publications and services programme.

This programme makes a clear distinction between general and specialist users and particular collections have been developed for these different groups. The collections *Press releases*, *Statistics in focus*, *Panorama of the European Union*, *Key indicators* and *Catalogues* are aimed at general users. They give immediate key information through analyses, tables, graphs and maps.

The collections *Methods and nomenclatures, Detailed tables* and *Studies and research* suit the needs of the specialist who is prepared to spend more time analysing and using very detailed information and tables.

All Eurostat products are disseminated through the Data Shop network or the sales agents of the Office for Official Publications of the European Communities. Data Shops are available in 12 of the 15 Member States as well as in Switzerland, Norway and the United States. They provide a wide range of services from simple database extracts to tailor-made investigations. The information is provided on paper and/or in electronic form via e-mail, on diskette or CD-ROM.

As part of the new programme Eurostat has developed its website. It includes a broad range of on-line information on Eurostat products and services, newsletters, catalogues, on-line publications as well as indicators on the euro-zone.

Yves Franchet
Director-General

For further information on Tourism Statistics, please refer to the following Eurostat publications :

- *Domestic Tourism up in Europe*: Statistics in Focus, 16/2001 (KS-NP-01-016-EN-C)
- *Tourism in the Mediterranean Partner Countries*: Statistics in Focus
- *Tourism trends in Mediterranean Countries* (KS-40-01-666-EN-C)
- *Tourism in Europe – Trends 1995-98*, 2000 (KS-28-00-591-EN-C)
- *Tourism in Europe – Key figures 1997-1998*, 1999 (CA-23-99-031-EN-C)
- *Tourism in the Central European Countries – Key figures 1997-1998*, 1999 (CA-23-99-047-EN-C)
- *Tourism in the Mediterranean Countries - Key Figures 1997-1998*, 1999 (CA-23-99-039-EN-C))
- *Yearbook on Tourism Statistics on CD-Rom–1994-1998 data*, 2001 (KS-34-00-495-3A-Z)
- *Euro-Mediterranean statistics*, 2-2000 (KS-DI-00-002-3U-C) *and 1-2001* (KS-DI-01-001-3U-C)
- *Community methodology on tourism statistics*, 1998 (CA-01-96-228-EN-C)

For general information on statistics produced at Community level, please refer to the Eurostat Catalogue (KS-36-01-637-FR-I) and to the internet site: http://europa.eu.int/comm/eurostat/.

For information on statistics in this publication, please contact Eurostat :
Hans-Werner Schmidt, Eurostat / D1
Tel. (352) 4301 34087, Fax (352) 4301 33899

For ordering publications and data extractions, please contact one of our Data shops (Luxembourg office Tel: (352) 43 35 22 51, Fax: (352) 43 35 22 221).

For information on Community activity in the field of Tourism, please refer to :

- *EU Schemes in support of tourism: an internet roadmap for the tourism sector,* DG ENTR, 2000.
- *Towards quality rural tourism: integrated quality management (IQM) of rural destinations,* Luxembourg: Eur-Op, 2000 (CT-24-99-041-**-C)
- *Towards quality coastal tourism: integrated quality management (IQM) of coastal tourist destinations:* Luxembourg: Eur-Op, 2000 (CT-24-99-057-**-C)
- *Towards quality urban tourism: integrated quality management (IQM) of urban tourist destinations,* Luxembourg: Eur-Op, 2000 (CT-24-99-049-**-C)
- *Conference proceedings "Tourism in the Information Society"* November 1999, DG XXIII, 1999 (online)

For further information on Community activity in the field of Tourism, please contact DG Enterprise:
Fax (32) 2 295 69 69, Internet site: http://europa.eu.int/comm/enterprise/index

This publication was prepared under the responsibility of:

François de Geuser, Head of Unit D1 "Classifications, Methodological Co-ordination; Registers, Information society, Tourism and Steel", Eurostat

General Co-ordination
Hans-Werner Schmidt *(Eurostat)*

European and Central European Countries chapters
Mathieu Mballa *(World Systems (Europe) Limited)*

Mediterranean countries chapters
Natalie Kirwan *(CESD-Madrid)*

Database management
Giuseppe Di Giacomo, Carlo Kirchen *(Eurostat)*

Data, Technical editing, Layout and composition
Jacqueline Genatzy *(World Systems (Europe) Limited)*

Acknowledgements

Eurostat gratefully acknowledge the valuable contributions of the following institutions:

Institut National de Statistique (Belgium)
Danmarks Statistik (Denmark)
Statistisches Bundesamt (Germany)
National Statistical Service (Greece)
Instituto Nacional de Estadística (Spain)
Instituto de Estudios Turísticos (Spain)
Institut National de la Statistique et des Etudes Economiques (France)
Ministère de l'Equipment, des Transports et du Tourisme, Direction du Tourisme (France)
Central Statistical Office (Ireland)
Statistics Iceland (Iceland)
Istituto Nazionale di Statistica (Italy)
Amt für Volkswirtschaft (Liechtenstein)
Service Central de la Statistique et des Etudes Economiques (Luxembourg)
Centraal Bureau voor de Statistiek (Netherlands)
Statistics Norway (Norway)
Österreichisches Statistisches Zentralamt (Austria)
Instituto Nacional de Estatistica (Portugal)
Office Fédéral de la Statistique (Switzerland)
Statistics Finland (Finland)
Statistics Sweden (Sweden)
Central Statistical Office (United Kingdom)
Department of Culture, Media and Sport (United Kingdom)

Institute of Statistics (Albania)
Federal Institute of Statistics (Bosnia and Herzegovina)
National Statistical Office (Bulgaria)
Central Bureau of Statistics (Croatia)
Czech Statistical Office (Czech Republic)

Statistical Office of Estonia (Estonia)
Statistical Office of Macedonia (Former Yugoslav Republic of Macedonia)
Hungarian Central Statistical Office (Hungary)
Central Statistical Bureau of Latvia (Latvia)
Lithuanian Department of Statistics (Lithuania)
Central Statistical Office of Poland (Poland)
National Commission for Statistics (Romania)
Statistical Office of the Slovak Republic (Slovakia)
Statistical Office of the Republic of Slovenia (Slovenia)

National Statistics Office and the Ministry of Tourism (Algeria)
Department of Statistics and Research and the Cyprus Tourism Organisation (Cyprus)
Central Agency for Public Mobilisation and Statistics (Egypt)
Central Bureau of Statistics (Israel)
Department of Statistics (Jordan)
Central Administration for Statistics and Ministry of Tourism (Lebanon)
Central Office of Statistics (Malta)
National Statistical Institute and the Ministry of Tourism (Morocco)
Central Bureau of Statistics (Palestine)
Central Bureau of Statistics (Syria)
National Statistical Institute and the Ministry of Tourism (Tunisia)
State Institute of Statistics and the Ministry of Tourism (Turkey)

The views expressed in the publication are those of the authors and do not necessarily reflect the opinion of the European Commission.

CONTENTS

TOURISM IN EUROPE

TOURISM IN THE CENTRAL EUROPEAN COUNTRIES

TOURISM IN THE MEDITERRANEAN COUNTRIES

Key statistics - 2000

Population	10 239 085
Surface area	39 500km²
Population density (inhabitants/km²)	259.2
Increase in GDP	4.0%
Exchange rate 1 EURO = BEF	40.3399
Increase of consumer price index	2.7%
Increase of hotels, cafés and restaurants consumer price index	2.9%

Recent trends

Little variation (-0.8%) was recorded in the number of hotels and similar establishments in 2000. The bed-places remained stable also (-0.2%). This stability came after a rise of 2.6% recorded in 1999.

2000 data on total overnight stays of tourists in collective accommodation establishments recorded an increase of 2.6% indicating a continuation of the positive trend of the previous year. This result is mostly due to a rise of 6.2% of the nights spent in hotels and similar establishments that largely offset the stability of the demand (-0.6%) recorded in other kinds of collective accommodation establishments. Resident nights spent grew by 4.4% breaking the negative trend of the previous years. Foreign tourist demand continued to rise in 2000 but at a moderate rate of 1% compared to 3.6% in 1999.

The deficit of the travel item of the Balance of Payments (referring to the Belgo-Luxembourg Economic Union-BLEU) grew by 9.2% in 2000. Though the travel receipts grew more than the travel expenditures (19.4% compared to 16.3%), the volume of the expenditures explained the increasing deficit. Travel receipts accounted for 17.4% of the credits of the services item of the Balance of Payments. Employment in the hotels and restaurants sector amounted to 136,000 persons recording an increase of 7.1% in 2000 with respect of 1999. The tourism sector represented 3.3% of total employment in 2000.

Key figures on tourism

Hotels and similar establishments

	1999	2000
Number of establishments	2 015	1 998
Number of bed-places	119 365	119 165
Average net rate of utilisation (%)	32.9	35.0

Nights spent in collective tourist accommodation (000s)

	1998	1999	2000
Total nights spent	28 023	28 477	29 215
Nights spent by residents	13 185	13 111	13 689
Nights spent by non-residents	14 838	15 366	15 526
of which: EU share (%)	83.6	84.1	82.9

Resident and non-resident shares of total nights spent in collective tourist accommodation - 2000

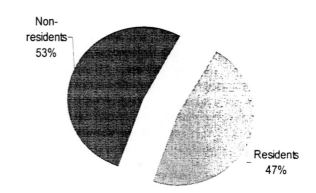

Non-residents 53%

Residents 47%

Balance of Payments* - Travel (Mio EURO)

	1998	1999	2000
Credits	4 869	6 610	7 891
Debits	7 889	9 462	11 004
Balance	-3 020	-2 852	-3 113

* Bleu= Belgo-Luxembourg Economic Union

Travel item in the Balance of Payments (Mio EURO)

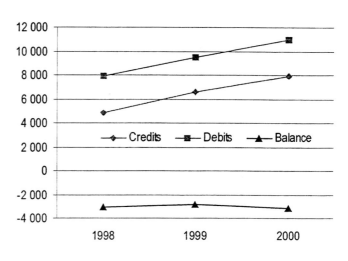

Total nights spent in collective tourist accommodation ('000)

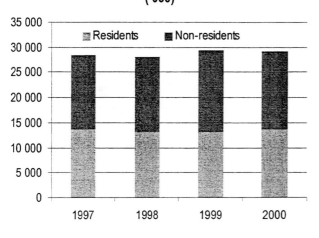

DENMARK

Key statistics - 2000

Population	5 330 020
Surface area	43 100 km²
Population density (inhabitants/km²)	123.6
Increase in GDP	2.9%
Exchange rate 1 EURO = DKK	7.45382
Increase of consumer price index	2.8%
Increase of hotels, cafés and restaurants consumer price index	3.0%

Recent trends

In 2000, there were 2 more hotels and similar establishments than in 1999 confirming the stability of the previous years. Bed-places grew by 2.6% in 2000.

The total nights spent in collective accommodation establishments remained stable (-0.1%) in 2000. This performance is due to the stability of foreign as well as domestic demand in collective accommodation establishments (with respectively +0.4% and –0.5% rates). Meanwhile, it is worth to note that the nights spent in hotels and similar establishments grew by 5.1% while the demand recorded in other kinds of collective establishments receded by 2.9%.

The deficit of the travel item of the Balance of Payments remained stable (+0.1%) in 2000. Though the travel receipts rose more than the travel expenditures (+29% compared to +21.4%), the volume of the expenditures explained the stability of the deficit. Travel receipts represented 19.8% of the credits of the Services item of the Balance of Payments in 2000.

Employment in hotels and restaurants grew by 4.6% in 2000 after declining by 12.2% in 1999. The HORECA sector accounted for 2.5% of total employment in 2000.

Key figures on tourism

Hotels and similar establishments

	1999	2000
Number of establishments	464	466
Number of bed-places	60 513	62 107
Average net rate of utilisation (%)	40.9	41.8

Nights spent in collective tourist accommodation (000s)

	1998	1999	2000
Total nights spent	25 171	25 212	25 174
Nights spent by residents	14 883	15 246	15 166
Nights spent by non-residents	10 288	9 966	10 008
of which: EU share (%)	74.0	73..2	72.5

Resident and non-resident shares of total nights spent in collective tourist accommodation - 2000

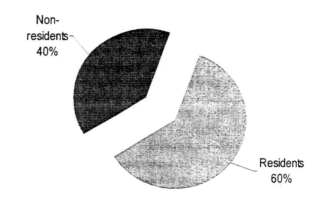

Balance of Payments - Travel (Mio EURO)

	1998	1999	2000
Credits	2 888	3 385	4 366
Debits	4 083	4 487	5 569
Balance	-1 195	-1 202	-1 203

Total nights spent in collective tourist accommodation ('000)

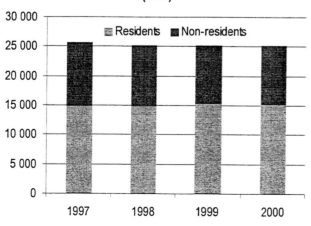

Travel item in the Balance of Payments (Mio EURO)

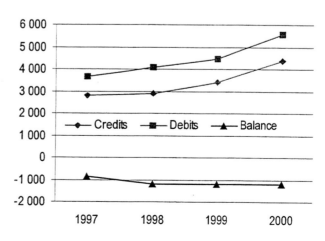

GERMANY

Key statistics - 2000

Population	82 163 475
Surface area	357 022km²
Population density (inhabitants/km²)	230.1
Increase in GDP	3.0%
Exchange rate 1 EURO = DEM	1.95583
Increase of consumer price index	2.0%
Increase of hotels, cafés and restaurants consumer price index	1.2%

Recent trends

In 2000, as in 1999 the number of hotels and similar establishments diminished slightly (-0.4% and -0.6% respectively). With a growth rate of 1.8%, the bed-places kept rising in 2000 continuing the positive trend of 1999 (+1.0%).

Total nights spent in collective tourist accommodation establishments continued to grow in 2000 at a higher rate of nearly 5% compared to 3.9% in 1999. The 2000 result is due to the rise of both domestic and inbound tourism. Resident nights grew by 4.2%, a rate higher than the 3.9% recorded in 1999. Foreign tourist demand rose at a significant rate of 10.1% coming after a rise of 3.8% recorded in 1999.

The deficit of the travel item of the Balance of Payments worsened by 4.6% in 2000. Though travel receipts grew more than travel expenditures (11.7% compared to 7%), the volume of the expenditures explained the increasing deficit. This volume made Germany the biggest outbound tourist market in the European Union with international travel expenditure representing almost three times the travel receipts in 2000. Nevertheless, travel receipts accounted for 20.3% of the credits of the services item of the Balance of Payments in 2000. In 2000, employment in the hotels and restaurants sector amounted to 1,210,000 persons, recording an increase of 4% with respect to 1999. The tourism sector represented 3.2% of total employment in 1999.

Total nights spent in collective tourist accommodation ('000)

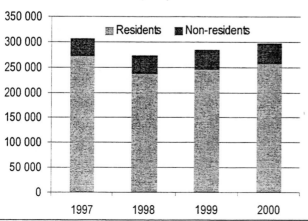

Key figures on tourism

Hotels and similar establishments

	1999	2000
Number of establishments	38 701	38 551
Number of bed-places	1 561 830	1 590 332
Average net rate of utilisation (%)	33.2	34.7

Nights spent in collective tourist accommodation (000s)

	1998	1999	2000
Total nights spent	273 759	284 356	298 488
Nights spent by residents	236 368	245 842	256 068
Nights spent by non-residents	37 091	38 515	42 420
of which: EU share (%)	57.7	58.4	56.6

Resident and non-resident shares of total nights spent in collective tourist accommodation - 2000

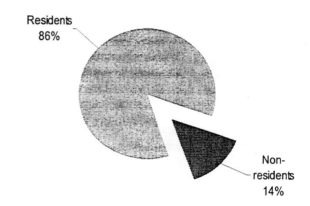

Balance of Payments - Travel (Mio EURO)

	1998	1999	2000
Credits	14 976	15 694	17 526
Debits	43 688	45 489	48 683
Balance	-28 712	-29 795	-31 157

Travel item in the Balance of Payments (Mio EURO)

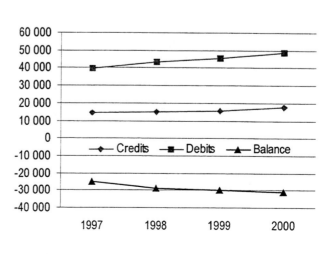

G R E E C E

Key statistics - 2000

Population	10 542 808
Surface area	132 000 km²
Population density (inhabitants/km²)	79.9
Increase in GDP	4.1%
Exchange rate 1 EURO = GRD	336.630
Increase of consumer price index	2.8%
Increase of hotels, cafés and restaurants consumer price index	4.6%

Recent trends

The number of hotels and similar establishments kept growing in 2000 at a lesser rate of 2.1% compared to 2.8% in 1999. The bed-places were also up by 1.6% indicating a continuation of the upward trend of the previous years.

The total nights spent in collective accommodation establishment grew by 1.4% continuing the upward trend of the previous years. Since resident nights spent declined by 1%, the 2000 result was due to the rise of 2.1% of foreign tourist demand. The drop of resident overnight stays in 2000 interrupted the upward trend of the previous years.

The surplus of the travel item of the Balance of Payments kept rising in 2000 but at a lesser rate of 12.6% compared to 14.6% in 1999. Despite a lower growth rate of +21.3% for travel receipts compared to +31.7% for travel expenditures, the volume of receipts explained the rise of the surplus in 2000. Travel receipts accounted for 48% of the credits of the Services item of the Balance of Payments.

In 2000, employment in HORECA sector remained stable and involved 253,000 persons. The HORECA sector represented 6.4% of total employment in 2000.

Total nights spent in collective tourist accommodation ('000)

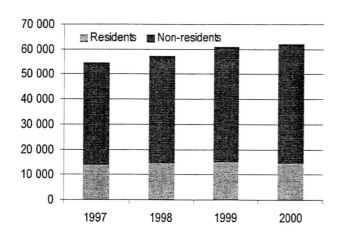

Key figures on tourism

Hotels and similar establishments

	1999	2000
Number of establishments	8 168	8 342
Number of bed-places	597 855	607 614
Average net rate of utilisation (%)	52.4	:

Nights spent in collective tourist accommodation (000s)

	1998	1999	2000
Total nights spent	57 411	61 170	62 009
Nights spent by residents	14 423	14 839	14 692
Nights spent by non-residents	42 989	46 330	47 316
Of which: EU share (%)	79.4	:	:

Resident and non-resident shares of total nights spent in collective tourist accommodation - 2000

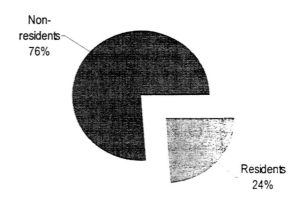

Balance of Payments - Travel (Mio EURO)

	1998	1999	2000
Credits	5 521	8 297	10 061
Debits	1 559	3 758	4 949
Balance	3 962	4 539	5112

Travel item in the Balance of Payments (Mio EURO)

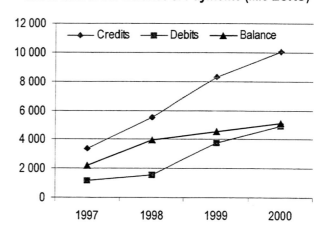

S P A I N

Key statistics - 2000

Population	39 441 679
Surface area	504 800km²
Population density (inhabitants/km²)	78.1
Increase in GDP	4.1%
Exchange rate 1 EURO = ESP	166.386
Increase of consumer price index	3.5%
Increase of hotels, cafés and restaurants consumer price index	4.3%

Recent trends

The number of hotels and similar establishments remained fairly stable (+0.4%) in 2000. The bed-places grew at a higher rate of 1.3%. In 2000, there were 58 more hotels and similar establishments than in 1999 offering altogether 16,676 more bed-places.

Total nights spent in hotels and similar establishments declined by 1.4% in 2000. This drop is attributable to a decline of 3.4% of foreign tourist demand. The resident nights rose by 2.3% continuing the positive trend of the previous years.

Spain enjoys the largest tourism foreign trade surplus among EU countries. The surplus of the travel item in the Balance of Payments kept rising in 2000 but at a lesser rate of 9.5% compared to 14% in 1999. The fall in the growth rate in 2000 was due to a fairly strong increase in travel expenditures (15.2%) and a lesser growth rate (+10.4%) of travel receipts. Travel credits accounted for more than half (58.8%) of the receipts of the services item of the Balance of Payments.

Employment in hotels and restaurants grew by 8.3% in 2000. The tourism sector employed 926,000 persons in 2000 representing 6.4% of total employment.

Total nights spent in hotels and similar establishments ('000)

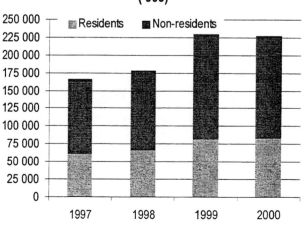

Key figures on tourism

Hotels and similar establishments

	1999	2000
Number of establishments	16 229	16 287
Number of bed-places	1 299 021	1 315 697
Average net rate of utilisation (%)	58.9	57.0

Nights spent in hotels and similar establishments (000s)

	*1998	1999	2000
Total nights spent	178 356	230 540	227 280
Nights spent by residents	66 552	81 504	83 350
Nights spent by non-residents	111 803	149 036	143 930
of which: EU share (%)	86.1	87.3	85.8

* Excludes 1* Hotels in 1998

Resident and non-resident shares of total nights spent in hotels and similar establishments - 2000

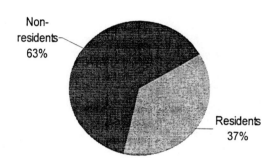

Balance of Payments - Travel (Mio EURO)

	1998	1999	2000
Credits	26 666	30 482	33 659
Debits	4 470	5 181	5 966
Balance	22 196	25 301	27 693

Travel item in the Balance of Payments (Mio EURO)

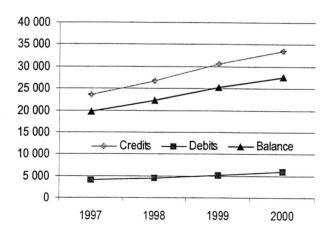

FRANCE

Key statistics - 2000

Population	59 225 683
Surface area	544 000 km²
Population density (inhabitants/km²)	108.9
Increase in GDP	3.1%
Exchange rate 1 EURO = FRF	6.55957
Increase of consumer price index	1.9%
Increase of hotels, cafés and restaurants consumer price index	1.9%

Recent trends

In 2000, the number of hotels and similar establishments remained stable (-0.3%) with 67 establishments less than in 1999. The number of bed-places totalled over 1.5 million, increasing by 1.6%.

Total nights spent in collective accommodation establishments continued to grow in 2000 but at a lesser rate of 1.2% compared to 6.4% in 1999. 2000 result is due to the rise of foreign tourist nights spent (+3.3%) since domestic demand remained stable (0.0%). The nights spent in hotels and similar establishments grew by 5.4% while the demand recorded in other kinds of collective accommodation establishments receded by 6%.

France continues to enjoy a substantial surplus foreign trade balance for tourism. The surplus of the travel item of the Balance of Payments kept growing in 2000 at a rate of 14.3% compared to 11.4% in 1999. This performance is due to a 9.7% rise of travel receipts combined with a growth at a lesser rate of 6.5% of travel expenditures. Travel receipts accounted for 38.2% of the credits of the services item of the Balance of Payments in 2000.

Employment in hotels and restaurants sector rose by 4.1% in 2000, amounting to 793 000 jobs. Tourism sector accounted for 3.4% of total employment.

Total nights spent in collective tourist accommodation ('000)

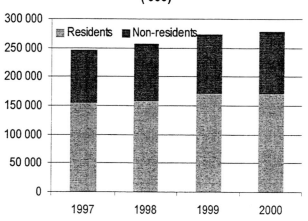

Key figures on tourism

Hotels and similar establishments

	1999	2000
Number of establishments	19 379	19 312
Number of bed-places	1 485 863	1 509 576
Average net rate of utilisation (%)	57.5	59.6

Nights spent in collective tourist accommodation (000s)

	1998	1999	2000
Total nights spent	258 192	274 686	278 103
Nights spent by residents	158 849	171 286	171 265
Nights spent by non-residents	99 343	103 400	106 838
of which: EU share (%)	72.2	79.0	:

Resident and non-resident shares of total nights spent in collective tourist accommodation - 2000

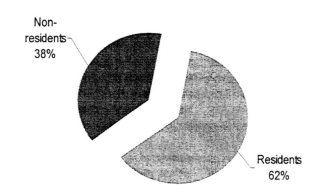

Balance of Payments - Travel (Mio EURO)

	1998	1999	2000
Credits	26 745	29 574	32 442
Debits	15 896	17 485	18 626
Balance	10 849	12 089	13 816

Travel item in the Balance of Payments (Mio EURO)

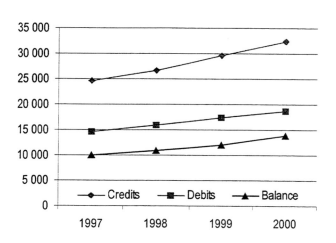

IRELAND

Key statistics - 2000

Population	3 776 577
Surface area	70 300km²
Population density (inhabitants/km²)	53.7
Increase in GDP	11.5%
Exchange rate 1 EURO = IEP	0.787564
Increase of consumer price index	5.2%
Increase of hotels, cafés and restaurants consumer price index	5.6%

Recent trends

The number of hotels and similar establishments decreased by 4.3% in 2000 breaking the positive trend of the three previous years. Bed-places followed a different pattern with a rise of 2.3% in 2000. However, this rate is less than the 15.6% increase recorded in 1999 or the 9.1% rise of 1998.

The total nights spent in collective accommodation establishments grew by 13.5% in 2000. With a positive growth rate of 19.7%, this result is mainly due to the rise of foreign tourist demand since resident overnight stays merely rose at a rate of 1.2%. Nights spent in hotels and similar establishments as well as the overnight stays in other types of collective establishments grew respectively by +11.4% and 21.4% in 2000.

The travel item in the Balance of Payments recorded a deficit in 2000. This deficit which amounted to EURO 34 million broke the trend of the surplus of the previous years. This result is due to a significant increase of 21.6% of the travel expenditures compared to a rise at a lesser rate of 15.8% of the travel receipts. However, these receipts accounted for 17% in the credits of the services item of the Balance of Payments.

Employment in hotels and restaurants sector grew by 4.9% in 2000 and involved 108,000 persons. The tourism sector represented 6.5% of total employment in 2000.

Total nights spent in collective tourist accommodation ('000)

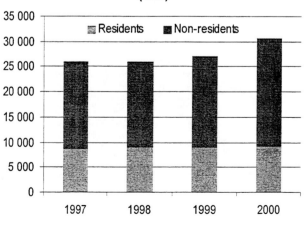

Key figures on tourism

Hotels and similar establishments

	1999	2000
Number of establishments	5 692	5 449
Number of bed-places	135 473	138 579
Average net rate of utilisation (%)	46.3	46.6

Nights spent in collective tourist accommodation (000s)

	1998	1999	2000
Total nights spent	26 023	27 077	30 738
Nights spent by residents	8 972	9 036	9 148
Nights spent by non-residents	17 051	18 041	21 590
of which: EU share (%)	:	:	:

Resident and non-resident shares of total nights spent in collective tourist accommodation - 2000

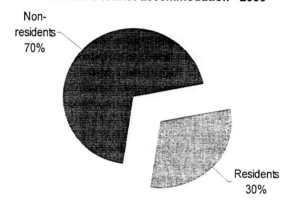

Balance of Payments - Travel (Mio EURO)

	1998	1999	2000
Credits	2 316	2 410	2 790
Debits	2 117	2 322	2 824
Balance	199	88	-34

Travel item in the Balance of Payments (Mio EURO)

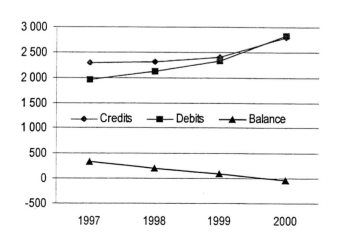

ITALY

Key statistics - 2000

Population	57 679 895
Surface area	301 300km²
Population density (inhabitants/km²)	191.4
Increase in GDP	2.9%
Exchange rate 1 EURO = ITL	1936.27
Increase of consumer price index	2.6%
Increase of hotels, cafés and restaurants consumer price index	3.2%

Recent trends

The number of hotels and similar establishments remained fairly stable in 2000 (-0.4%), but continuing the slow regression of the past years. This stability has lasted since 1997. The bed-places followed a different pattern with a positive growth rate of 1.5% in 2000 coming after a comparable rise (+1.4%) in 1999.Total nights spent in collective accommodation establishments grew significantly by 7.8% in 2000. This rate is more than the double of the 2.9% recorded in 1999 or the 2.5% rise of 1998. In hotels and similar establishments as well as other kinds of collective accommodation establishments nights spent grew respectively by 3.9% and 17.2%. Resident nights spent went up by 7.2%, a rate more than triple that recorded in 1999 (1.9%). Foreign tourist demand grew significantly by 8.6% compared to 4.5% in 1999.

The surplus of the travel item in the Balance of Payments jumped by 20.7% after being stable (-0.7%) in 1999. The 2000 result is due to a rise of 11.6% in the travel receipts that completely offset the 5.4% growth of tourism expenditures. In 2000 tourism receipts accounted for 48.3% in the credits of the services item of the Balance of Payments. Employment in hotels and restaurants sector amounted to 773,000 persons recording an increase of 4.2% in 2000 with respect of 1999. The tourism sector represented 3.7% of total employment in 2000.

Total nights spent in collective tourist accommodation ('000)

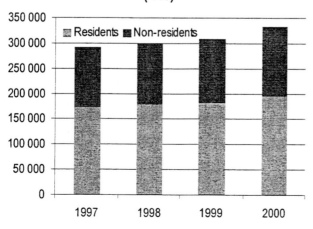

Key figures on tourism

Hotels and similar establishments

	1999	2000
Number of establishments	33 379	33 244
Number of bed-places	1 807 275	1 834 423
Average net rate of utilisation (%)	39.6	39.0

Nights spent in collective tourist accommodation (000s)

	1998	1999	2000
Total nights spent	299 508	308 315	332 358
Nights spent by residents	178 266	181 647	194 813
Nights spent by non-residents	121 242	126 668	137 545
of which: EU share (%)	69.6	70.0	:

Resident and non-resident shares of total nights spent in collective tourist accommodation - 2000

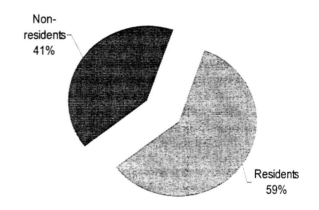

Non-residents 41%

Residents 59%

Balance of Payments - Travel (Mio EURO)

	1998	1999	2000
Credits	26 640	26 716	29 823
Debits	15 707	15 858	16 718
Balance	10 933	10 858	13 105

Travel item in the Balance of Payments (Mio EURO)

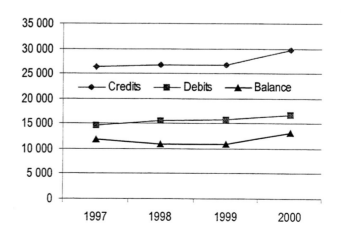

LUXEMBOURG

Key statistics - 2000

Population	435 700
Surface area	2 586km²
Population density (inhabitants/km²)	168.4
Increase in GDP	8.5%
Exchange rate 1 EURO = LUF	40.3399
Increase of consumer price index	3.8%
Increase of hotels, cafés and restaurants consumer price index	2.6%

Recent trends

The number of hotels and similar establishments continued to decline in 2000 but at a lesser rate of 1.8% compared to 5% in 1999. The bed-places remained stable (-0.2%) after a drop of 1.8% in the previous year.

The total nights spent in collective tourist accommodation establishments decreased by 6% in 2000 interrupting the growth (+5.2%) of 1999. Resident nights (-14.3%) as well as non-resident overnight stays (-5.2%) decreased in 2000. Tourist demand in terms of total nights spent for hotels and similar establishments remained stable (+0.4%) while a drop of 11.2% was recorded in the nights spent in other kinds of collective tourist accommodation establishments.

The deficit of the travel item of the Balance of Payments (referring to the Belgo-Luxembourg Economic Union-BLEU) grew by 9.2% in 2000. Though the travel receipts grew more than the travel expenditures (19.4% compared to 16.3%), the volume of the expenditures explained the increasing deficit. Travel receipts accounted for 17.4% of the credits of the services item of the Balance of Payments.

Employment in hotels and restaurants sector numbered 9,000 persons in 2000. The tourism sector represented 3.4% of the total employment in 1999.

Total nights spent in collective tourist accommodation ('000)

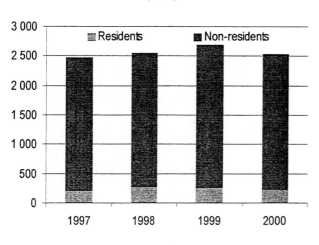

Key figures on tourism

Hotels and similar establishments

	1999	2000
Number of establishments	325	319
Number of bed-places	14 449	14 415
Average net rate of utilisation (%)	25.4	26.0

Nights spent in collective tourist accommodation (000s)

	1998	1999	2000
Total nights spent	2 561	2 694	2 532
Nights spent by residents	265	254	218
Nights spent by non-residents	2 296	2 440	2 314
of which: EU share (%)	89.7	90.2	89.4

Resident and non-resident shares of total nights spent in collective tourist accommodation - 2000

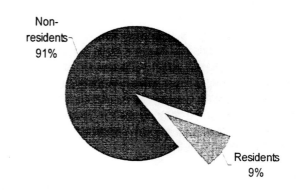

Balance of Payments* - Travel (Mio EURO)

	1998	1999	2000
Credits	4 869	6 610	7 891
Debits	7 889	9 462	11 004
Balance	-3 020	-2 852	-3 113

* Bleu= Belgo-Luxembourg Economic Union

Travel item in the Balance of Payments (Mio EURO)

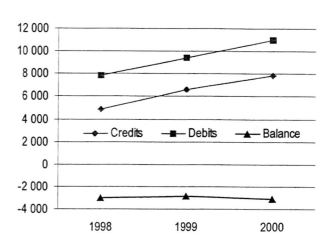

Key statistics - 2000

Population	15 863 950
Surface area	41 200km²
Population density (inhabitants/km²)	385
Increase in GDP	3.9%
Exchange rate 1 EURO = NLG	2.20371
Increase of consumer price index	2.3%
Increase of hotels, cafés and restaurants consumer price index	3.5%

Recent trends

In 2000, there were 9 more hotels and similar establishments than in 1999 (+0.3%) offering a total of 3,317 more bed-places (+1.4%).

The total nights spent in collective accommodation establishments remained stable (-0.6%) in 2000 interrupting the positive trend of the previous years. This stability is due to a rise in total nights spent of 3% recorded in hotels and similar establishments combined with a drop of 2.6% in other kinds of collective accommodation establishments. Stability also characterises the figures referring to domestic (-0.9%) and inbound (-0.1%) tourism. 2000 followed the good year of 1999 when domestic tourism grew by 7.9% and inbound tourism by 11.8%, compared to 1998.

In 2000, the deficit of the travel item of the Balance of Payments substantially worsened by 60.6%. This result is mainly due to a high growth rate of 34.5% of the travel expenditures coming after a much lower rate of increase in 1999 (3.4%). Travel receipts also grew in 2000 but at a lesser rate of 20.8%. These receipts accounted for 14% of the credits of the services item of the Balance of Payments.

In 2000, employment in hotels and restaurants sector amounted to 286,000 persons recording an increase of 13% with respect of 1999. The tourism sector accounted for 3.4% of the total employment in 1999.

Total nights spent in collective tourist accommodation ('000)

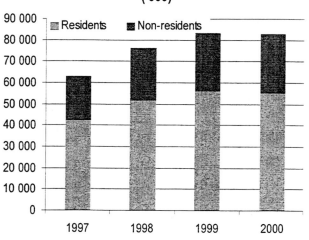

Key figures on tourism

Hotels and similar establishments

	1999	2000
Number of establishments	2 826	2 835
Number of bed-places	169 749	173 066
Average net rate of utilisation (%)	48.0	:

Nights spent in collective tourist accommodation (000s)

	1998	1999	2000
Total nights spent	76 322	83 298	82 771
Nights spent by residents	51 749	55 823	55 310
Nights spent by non-residents	24 573	27 475	27 461
of which: EU share (%)	77.2	77.5	76.4

Resident and non-resident shares of total nights spent in collective tourist accommodation - 2000

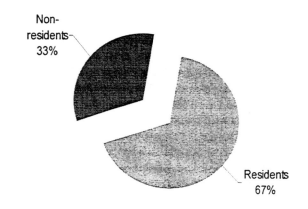

Balance of Payments - Travel (Mio EURO)

	1998	1999	2000
Credits	6 081	6 590	7 962
Debits	9 716	10 043	13 506
Balance	-3 635	-3 453	-5 544

Travel item in the Balance of Payments (Mio EURO)

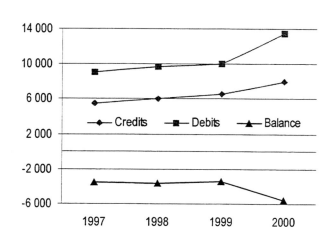

AUSTRIA

Key statistics - 2000

Population	8 102 557
Surface area	83 900km²
Population density (inhabitants/km²)	96.6
Increase in GDP*	3.2%
Exchange rate 1 EURO = ATS	13.7603
Increase of consumer price index	2.0%
Increase of hotels, cafés and restaurants consumer price index	2.1%

Estimate

Recent trends

The number of hotels and similar establishments grew by 3.2% in 2000 after a drop of 2.6% in 1999 compared to the previous year. Bed-places followed the same pattern with a growth rate of 9% in 2000 after a drop of 1.4% in 1999.

The total nights spent in collective tourist accommodation rose by 1.6% confirming the upward trend of 1999. Resident nights as well as non-resident overnight stays went up by 3% and 1% respectively. In terms of total nights spent, hotels and similar establishments increased their activity by 1.8% while a growth rate of 0.7% was recorded for other kinds of collective accommodation establishments.

The surplus of the travel item of the balance of payments decreased by 18.6% in 2000. This result is due to a higher growth rate of travel expenditures (+8.6%) compared to travel receipts (+4%). In the Balance of Payments, travel receipts accounted for 35.7% of total international service receipts.

In 2000, employment in hotels and restaurants sector grew by 2.9%. The tourism sector employed 215,000 persons representing 5.8% of the total employment.

Total nights spent in collective tourist accommodation ('000)

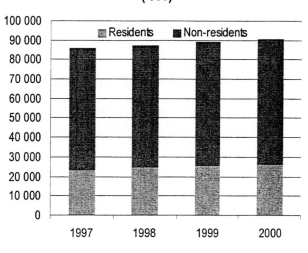

Key figures on tourism

Hotels and similar establishments

	1999	2000
Number of establishments	15 378	15 865
Number of bed-places	576 602	628 208
Average net rate of utilisation (%)	36.1%	35.7%

Nights spent in collective tourist accommodation (000s)

	1998	1999	2000
Total nights spent	87 625	89 297	90 711
Nights spent by residents	24 426	25 466	26 242
Nights spent by non-residents	63 199	63 831	64 469
of which: EU share (%)	85.5	85.8	84.9

Resident and non-resident shares of total nights spent in collective tourist accommodation - 2000

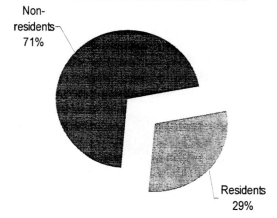

Balance of Payments - Travel (Mio EURO)

	1998	1999	2000
Credits	9 985	10 333	10 746
Debits	8 496	8 571	9 312
Balance	1 489	1 762	1 434

Travel item in the Balance of Payments (Mio EURO)

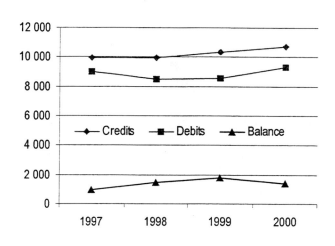

PORTUGAL

Key statistics - 2000

Population	9 997 590
Surface area	92 400 km²
Population density (inhabitants/km²)	108.2
Increase in GDP	3.3%
Exchange rate 1 EURO = PTE	200.482
Increase of consumer price index	2.8%
Increase of hotels, cafés and restaurants consumer price index	3.7%

Recent trends

The number of hotels and similar establishments remained fairly stable (-1.0%) in 2000. The bed-places rose by 1.4% continuing the upward trend of the previous years.

In 1999, the total nights spent in collective accommodation establishments rose by 1.8%. Since non-resident overnight stays remained stable (-0.8%), 1999 result was mainly due to the rise of 6% of domestic demand. The nights spent in hotels and similar establishments as well as the demand recorded in other kinds of collective accommodation establishments grew respectively by 1% and 4.9% in 1999.

The surplus of the travel item of the Balance of Payments grew significantly by 24.9% in 2000. Though travel expenditures rose by 14.1%, travel receipts grew at a higher rate of 20.1% explaining 2000 result. Travel receipts accounted for 63.3% of the credits of the services item of the Balance of Payments.

Employment in hotels and restaurants sector remained stable (+0.8%) and amounted to 254,000 persons in 2000. HORECA represented 5.2% of total employment in 2000.

Total nights spent in collective tourist accommodation ('000)

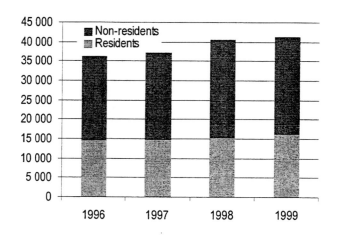

Key figures on tourism

Hotels and similar establishments

	1999	2000
Number of establishments	1 772	1 755
Number of bed-places	216 828	219 854
Average net rate of utilisation (%)	44.0	44.6

Nights spent in collective tourist accommodation (000s)

	1998	1999	2000
Total nights spent	40 599	41 323	:
Nights spent by residents	15 326	16 243	:
Nights spent by non-residents	25 273	25 080	:
of which: EU share (%)	87.7	87.3	:

Resident and non-resident shares of total nights spent in collective tourist accommodation - 1999

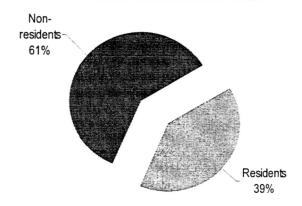

Balance of Payments - Travel (Mio EURO)

	1998	1999	2000
Credits	4 737	4 814	5 783
Debits	2 072	2 126	2 426
Balance	2 665	2 688	3 357

Travel item in the Balance of Payments (Mio EURO)

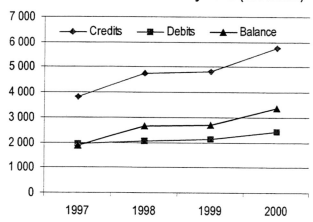

FINLAND

Population	5 171 302
Surface area	337 100km²
Population density (inhabitants/km²)	15.3
Increase in GDP	5.7%
Exchange rate 1 EURO = FIM	5.94573
Increase of consumer price index	3.0%
Increase of hotels, cafés and restaurants consumer price index	3.0%

Recent trends

In 2000, there were 7 more hotels and similar establishments than in 1999 (+0.7%) offering a total of 2,430 more bed-places (+2.1%).

Total nights spent in collective accommodation establishments rose at a higher rate of 3% compared to 1.6% in 1999. Since the nights spent in other kinds of collective accommodation establishments remained stable (-0.5%), 2000 performance was essentially due to a rise of 3.7% of nights spent in hotels and similar establishments for which foreign tourist demand grew by 8.9%. Resident overnight stays in hotels and similar establishments were also up (+1.5%) in 2000, at exactly the same rate as in 1999.

The deficit of the travel item of the Balance of Payments increased by 15.3% in 2000 confirming the negative trend of the previous years. 2000 result is due to a drop of travel receipts (1.2%) combined with a rise of travel expenditures (2.9%). Both figures indicated a continuation of the trend of 1999 and 1998. Travel receipts represented approximately 21.5% of the credits of the services item of the Balance of Payments. Employment in the hotels and restaurants sector remained stable in 2000. The tourism sector employed 78,000 persons representing 3.3% of total employment.

Total nights spent in collective tourist accommodation ('000)

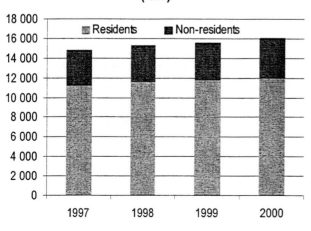

Key figures on tourism

Hotels and similar establishments

	1999	2000
Number of establishments	1 004	1 011
Number of bed-places	114 892	117 322
Average net rate of utilisation (%)	37.4	36.9

Nights spent in collective tourist accommodation (000s)

	1998	1999	2000
Total nights spent	15 327	15 578	16 042
Nights spent by residents	11 627	11 804	11 976
Nights spent by non-residents	3 700	3 774	4 066
of which: EU share (%)	53.4	56.5	55.1

Resident and non-resident shares of total nights spent in collective tourist accommodation - 2000

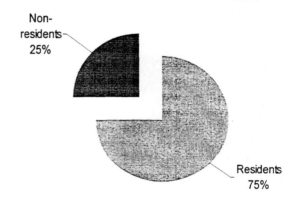

Balance of Payments - Travel (Mio EURO)

	1998	1999	2000
Credits	1 456	1 434	1 417
Debits	1 843	1 910	1 966
Balance	-387	-476	-549

Travel item in the Balance of Payments (Mio EURO)

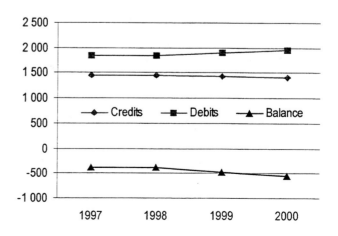

SWEDEN

Key statistics - 2000

Population	8 861 426
Surface area	450 000km²
Population density (inhabitants/km²)	19.7
Increase in GDP	3.6%
Exchange rate 1 EURO = SEK	8.44519
Increase of consumer price index	1.4%
Increase of hotels, cafés and restaurants consumer price index	1.5%

Recent trends

Little variation can be observed in 2000 compared to 1999. The number of hotels and similar establishments remained stable (+0.4%).

Data for the total nights spent in collective accommodation establishments remained at the same level (0.1%). Stability also characterises the figures of resident nights (0.3%) as well as those of non-resident overnight stays (0.6%). These figures contrast with the rise recorded in 1999 compared to 1998: +7.1% for non-resident nights and +6.1% for resident nights. In 2000, total tourist nights spent in hotels and similar establishments rose by 2.7% while the other kind of collective accommodation establishments recorded a drop of 3.1%.

The deficit of the travel item of the Balance of Payments increased by 8.7% in 2000 indicating a continuation of a trend of the previous years. This performance is explained by a higher growth rate of travel expenditures (6.2%) compared to a lesser rise of travel receipts (+3.8%). International travel earnings accounted for 20.7% of services' receipts in the Balance of Payments.

In 2000, employment in hotels and restaurants sector grew by 6.4%. The tourism sector employed 117,000 persons accounting for 2.8% of total employment.

Total nights spent in collective tourist accommodation ('000)

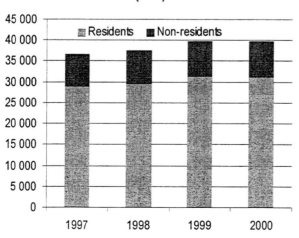

Key figures on tourism

Hotels and similar establishments

	1999	2000
Number of establishments	1 898	1 906
Number of bed-places	184 970	188 289
Average net rate of utilisation (%)	34.1	:

Nights spent in collective tourist accommodation (000s)

	1998	1999	2000
Total nights spent	37 497	39 855	39 809
Nights spent by residents	29 468	31 254	31 155
Nights spent by non-residents	8 029	8 601	8 654
of which: EU share (%)	57.4	54.4	54.7

Resident and non-resident shares of total nights spent in collective tourist accommodation - 2000

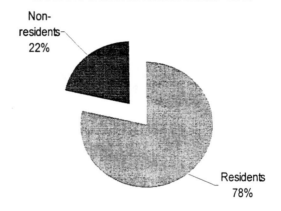

Balance of Payments - Travel (Mio EURO)

	1998	1999	2000
Credits	3 738	3 888	4 037
Debits	6 891	7 532	7 999
Balance	-3 153	-3 644	-3 962

Travel item in the Balance of Payments (Mio EURO)

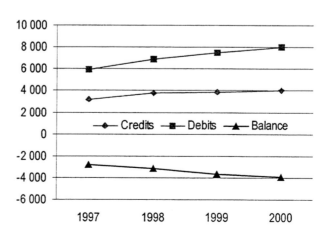

UNITED KINGDOM

Key statistics - 2000

Population	59 623 406
Surface area	244 100 km²
Population density (inhabitants/km²)	244.2
Increase in GDP	3.1%
Exchange rate 1 EURO = GBP	0.609478
Increase of consumer price index	0.8%
Increase of hotels, cafés and restaurants consumer price index	3.2%

Recent trends

In 2000, the number of hotels and similar establishments decreased by 1.5% breaking the positive trend of the previous years. Bed-places followed the same pattern with a drop of 1.9% recorded in 2000.

The total nights spent in collective accommodation establishments kept growing in 2000 at nearly the same rate as 1999 (9% compared to 8.9% in 1999). 2000 result was due to the rise of 13% of resident nights spent since foreign tourist demand remained globally stable (-0.5%). Hotels and similar establishments increased significantly their overnight stays at a higher rate of 32.9% compared to +8.3% recorded in 1999. The nights spent in other kinds of collective accommodation establishments declined by 21.5% in 2000.

The deficit of the travel item of the Balance of Payments kept growing in 2000 (+ 39.2% compared to 45.2% in 1999). 2000 result is explained by the rise of travel expenditures at a higher growth rate of +20.1% compared to +8.9% for travel receipts. However, travel receipts accounted for 21.6% of the credits of the services item of the Balance of Payments. Employment in hotels and restaurants sector declined by 1.3% in 2000 amounting to 1 139 thousands jobs. The tourism sector represented 4.1% of total employment in 2000.

Total nights spent in collective tourist accommodation ('000)

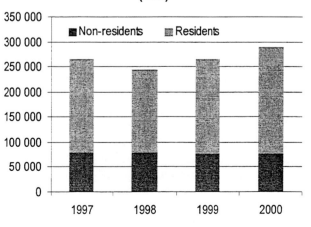

Key figures on tourism

Hotels and similar establishments

	1999	2000
Number of establishments	51 300	50 549
Number of bed-places	1 176 490	1 154 580
Average net rate of utilisation (%)	42.4	43.0

Nights spent in collective tourist accommodation (000s)

	1998	1999	2000
Total nights spent	243 842	265 431	289 345
Nights spent by residents	164 983	187 830	212 160
Nights spent by non-residents	78 859	77 601	77 185
of which: EU share (%)	42.2	44.7	:

Resident and non-resident shares of total nights spent in collective tourist accommodation - 2000

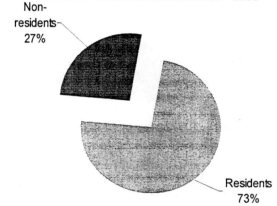

Balance of Payments - Travel (Mio EURO)

	1998	1999	2000
Credits	21 135	21 757	23 695
Debits	29 881	34 452	41 362
Balance	-8 746	-12 695	-17 667

Travel item in the Balance of Payments (Mio EURO)

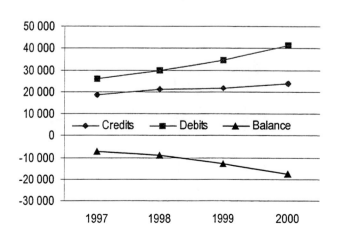

ICELAND

Key statistics - 2000

Population	279 048
Surface area	103 000 km^2
Population density (inhabitants/km^2)	2.7
Increase in GDP*	3.6%
Exchange rate 1 EURO = ISK	72.5848
Increase of consumer price index	:
Increase of hotels, cafés and restaurants consumer price index	:

* estimates

Recent trends

With one more unit, hotels and similar establishments remained fairly stable (+0.4%) in 1999 compared to 1998. The number of bed-places 1999 remained at the same level as in 1998 after a significant rise of 12.3% recorded in 1998.

The total nights spent in collective accommodation establishments amounted to 1.5 million in 1998. Inbound tourism represented 59% of total nights spent. EU 15 resident demand accounted for 73.7% of foreign tourist overnight stays. Hotels and similar establishments' share amounted to 73.6% of total overnight stays in collective accommodation in 1998.

The deficit of the travel item of the Balance of Payments was reduced by 8.4% in 2000 breaking the trend of the previous years. The drop of travel expenditures at a higher rate of -6.3% compared to -4.3% for travel receipts explains this result. Travel receipts accounted for 21.5% of the credits of the services item of the Balance of Payments.

Employment in hotels and restaurants sector rose by 40% in 2000 continuing the upward trend of the previous years. 7,000 persons were employed in tourism sector representing 4.5% of total employment in 2000.

Total nights spent in collective tourist accommodation ('000)

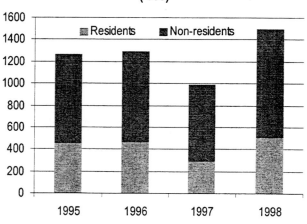

Key figures on tourism

Hotels and similar establishments

	1999	2000
Number of establishments	254	:
Number of bed-places	12030	:
Average net rate of utilisation (%)	:	:

Nights spent in collective tourist accommodation (000s)

	1998	1999	2000
Total nights spent	1 496	:	:
Nights spent by residents	506	:	:
Nights spent by non-residents	990	:	:
of which: EU share (%)	73.7	:	:

Resident and non-resident shares of total nights spent in collective tourist accommodation - 1998

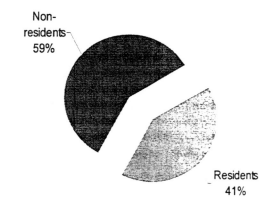

Balance of Payments - Travel (Mio EURO)

	1998	1999	2000
Credits	183	208	199
Debits	352	410	384
Balance	-169	-202	-185

Travel item in the Balance of Payments (Mio EURO)

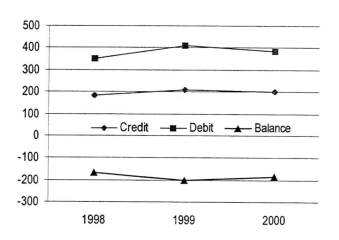

LIECHTENSTEIN

Key statistics - 2000

Population*	32 015
Surface area	160 km²
Population density (inhabitants/km²)	200
Increase in GDP	:
Exchange rate 1 EURO = CHF	:
Increase of consumer price index	:
Increase of hotels, cafés and restaurants consumer price index	:

* 1999 data

Recent trends

There were 52 hotels and similar establishments in Liechtenstein in 1998 giving a total number of 1 385 bed-places.

Compared to 1998, total nights spent in collective accommodation establishments in 2000 indicate a rise of 7.2%. This result confirmed the upward trend of the previous years. In 2000, resident demand as well as foreign tourist overnight stays grew respectively by 38.2% and 4.6% compared to 1998.

In hotels and similar establishments, resident nights spent continued to grow at a rate of 7.5% in 2000 compared to 1999. This rise came after a drop of 17.1% recorded in 1999.

Non-resident overnight stays in hotels and similar establishments grew by 7.5% compared to 1999 continuing the upward trend of the previous years. In 2000, foreign tourist demand accounted for 90% of total nights spent in collective accommodation establishments.

In 2000 nights spent by EU 15 tourists grew by 9.2% compared to 1998 and accounted for 58.6% of foreign tourist demand.

In 1997, the surplus of the travel item of the Balance of Payments (referring to Switzerland and Liechtenstein) amounted to ECU 1,089 million.

Key figures on tourism

Hotels and similar establishments

	1998	1999	2000
Number of establishments	52	:	:
Number of bed-places	1 385	:	:
Average net rate of utilisation (%)	27.0	28.3	30.6

Nights spent in collective tourist accommodation (000s)

	1998	1999*	2000
Total nights spent	174	124	187
Nights spent by residents	14	3	19
Nights spent by non-residents	160	121	168
of which: EU share (%)	56.1	:	58.6

* only Hotels and Similar Establishments

Resident and non-resident shares of total nights spent in collective tourist accommodation - 2000

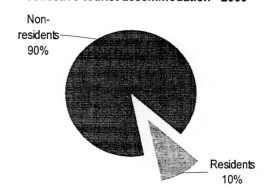

Total nights spent in collective tourist accommodation ('000)

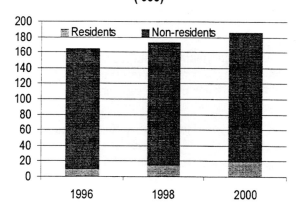

EⅦ/
eurostat

Key statistics - 2000

Population	4 478 497
Surface area	323 758km²
Population density (inhabitants/km²)	13.8
Increase in GDP	2.3%
Exchange rate 1 EURO = NOK	8.11292
Increase of consumer price index	:
Increase of hotels, cafés and restaurants consumer price index	:

(*)estimates

Recent trends

The number of hotels and similar establishments remained fairly stable (+0.3%) in 2000 breaking the declining trend of the previous years. The bed-places grew by 2.4% confirming the upward trend of the previous years.

The total nights spent in collective accommodation establishments showed stability (-0.7%) in 2000 as in 1999 (+0.2%). The demand recorded in hotels and similar establishments decreased by 1% while the nights spent in other kinds of collective accommodation establishments remained stable (-0.1%). Non-resident nights spent declined significantly by 4.4% while domestic tourists' demand grew by 1% in 2000.

The deficit of the travel item of the Balance of Payments was reduced by 19.4% in 1999. Though a drop of travel receipts (-11.6%) was recorded, travel expenditures decreased at a higher rate of -15.8% explaining the 1999 result. In 1999, travel receipts represented 17.1% of the credits of the services item of the Balance of Payments.

In 2000, employment in HORECA sector amounted to 74,000 persons, recording an increase of 1.4% with respect to 1999. The tourism sector accounted for 3.3% of total employment in 2000.

Total nights spent in collective tourist accommodation ('000)

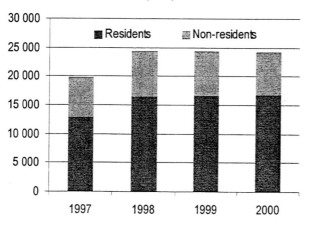

Key figures on tourism

Hotels and similar establishments

	1999	2000
Number of establishments	1 162	1 166
Number of bed-places	137 653	141 000
Average net rate of utilisation (%)	38.1	36.8

Nights spent in collective tourist accommodation (000s)

	1998	1999	2000
Total nights spent	24 383	24 443	24 270
Nights spent by residents	16 514	16 628	16 801
Nights spent by non-residents	7 869	7 815	7 469
of which: EU share (%)	82.8	81.3	81.0

Resident and non-resident shares of total nights spent in collective tourist accommodation - 2000

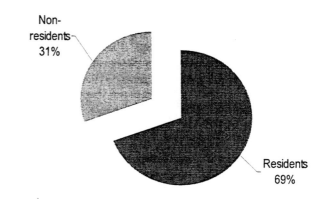

Balance of Payments - Travel (Mio EURO)

	1998	1999	2000
Credits	1 868	1 652	:
Debits	4 065	3 423	:
Balance	-2 197	-1 771	:

Travel item in the Balance of Payments (Mio EURO)

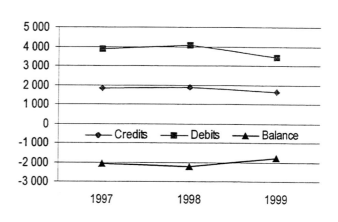

SWITZERLAND

Key statistics - 2000

Population	7 164 444
Surface area	41 284 km²
Population density (inhabitants/km²)	173.5
Increase in GDP	3.4%
Exchange rate 1 EURO = CHF	1.55786
Increase of consumer price index	:
Increase of hotels, cafés and restaurants consumer price index	:

Recent trends

The number of hotels and similar establishments declined by 0.4% in 2000 indicating a slowing down of the contraction experienced over the previous years. The bed-places followed the same pattern recording a significant drop of 15.8% in 2000.

In 1999, the total nights spent in collective accommodation establishments declined slightly (-0.7%) compared to 1998. Since foreign tourist demand declined by 1.2%, 1999 result was mainly explained by the stability (-0.2%) of resident overnight stays.

EU 15 residents accounted for 79.4% of foreign tourist overnight stays. The nights spent in hotels and similar establishment increased only very slightly (+0.9%), while the demand recorded in other kinds of collective accommodation establishments declined by 2.1%.

In 1997, the surplus of the travel item of the Balance of Payments (referring to Switzerland and Liechtenstein) amounted to ECU 1,089 million.

Employment in hotels and restaurants sector grew by 5.4% in 2000 and amounted to 118,000 persons. This rise came after a drop of 4.3% recorded in 1999 with respect of 1998. HORECA accounted for 3% of total employment in 2000.

Key figures on tourism

Hotels and similar establishments

	1999	2000
Number of establishments	5 826	5 800
Number of bed-places	260 592	219 394
Average net rate of utilisation (%)	:	42.3

Nights spent in collective tourist accommodation (000s)

	1998	1999	2000
Total nights spent	67 794	67 340	:
Nights spent by residents	35 557	35 477	:
Nights spent by non-residents	32 237	31 863	:
of which: EU share (%)	79.6	79.4	:

Resident and non-resident shares of total nights spent in collective tourist accommodation – 2000

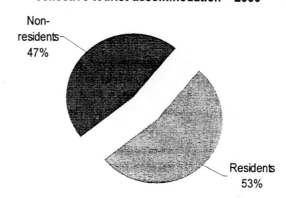

Non-residents 47%

Residents 53%

Total nights spent in collective tourist accommodation ('000)

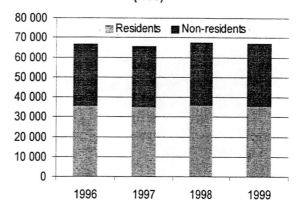

Key statistics - 2000

Population	3 410 200
Surface area	28 748 km²
Population density (inhabitants/km²)	8.4
Increase in GDP	7.8
Exchange rate 1 EURO = ALL	135.478
Increase of consumer price index	4.2
Increase of hotels, cafés and restaurants consumer price index	5.9

Recent trends

The hotels and similar establishments grew by 18.3% in 2000 continuing the upward trend of the previous years. The bed-places continued their serrated evolution recording a significant increase of 65.6% in 2000 after a drop of 31.4% in 1999.

In 2000, the nights spent in hotels and similar establishments grew by 51.8% indicating a continuation of the upward trend of the previous years. This result is mostly due to a significant rise of 91.4% of domestic tourism since foreign tourist overnight stays merely grew by 2.5%. The share of non-resident in the nights spent in hotels and similar establishment is decreasing since 1997 (from 61.1% in 1997 to 30% in 2000).

Arrivals of visitors at the borders decreased by 14.5% in 2000. In 1999, tourists accounted for 95.4% of the visitors.
The surplus of the travel item of the Balance of Payments decreased by 35.4% in 2000. Though the travel receipts grew by 107.5%, travel expenditures rose from 11.1 to 290.5 millions of Euro (+2470.8%). Travel receipts as well as travel expenditures continued in 2000 the upward trend of the previous years.

In 2000, employment in hotels and restaurants sector amounted to 19,003 persons, recording an increase of 35.7% with respect of 1999.

Total nights spent in hotels and similar establishments ('000)

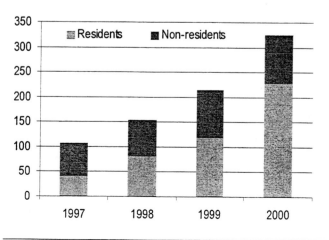

Key figures on tourism

Hotels and similar establishments

	1999	2000
Number of establishments	103	142
Number of bed-places	3 575	5 919
Average net rate of utilisation (%)	20.0	29.0

Nights spent in hotels and similar establishments (000s)

	1998	1999	2000
Total nights spent	154	215	326
Nights spent by residents	81	119	228
Nights spent by non-residents	73	96	98
of which: EU share (%)	63.0		

Resident and non-resident shares of total nights spent in hotels and similar establishments - 2000

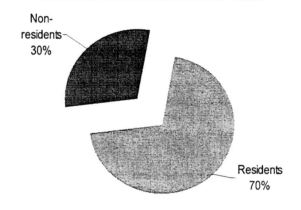

Arrivals at the borders ('000)

	1998	1999	2000
Visitors	184	371	317
Tourists	:	354	

Balance of Payments - Travel (Mio EURO)

	1998	1999	2000
Credits	48	198	411
Debits	4	11	291
Balance	42	187	121

Travel item in the Balance of Payments (Mio EURO)

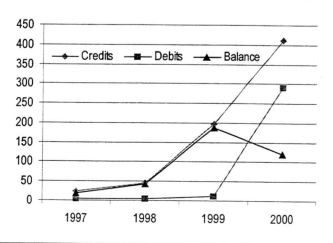

BOSNIA AND HERZEGOVINA

Population	2.8 million
Surface area	26 110 km^2
Population density (inhabitants/km^2)	107
Increase in GDP	15.7%
Exchange rate 1 EURO = BAM	1.97
Increase of consumer price index	5.1%
Increase of hotels, cafés and restaurants consumer price index	:

Recent trends

1995-1998 data on the number of establishments and the number of bed-places in hotels and similar establishments show a positive trend. The number of establishments increased by 34% in 1998 after a remarkable increase in 1997, when the number of establishments more than doubled (108.3%). In 1996 they increased by 26.3%. Figures on the number of bed-places follow a similar pattern; 1998 data show a modest growth (3.3%) in comparison to that of 1997, when the number of bed-places rose by 127.3%. In 1996 the number of bed-places grew by 42%.

Total nights spent in all collective accommodation establishments also reveal a positive trend. 1998 data show a growth rate of 9.6% in total nights spent. The growth rate, which in 1996 reached 137.1%, diminished to 40.3% in 1997. Both the nights spent by residents and non-residents follow the same trend while the latter presents a milder growth pattern.

Total nights spent in collective tourist accommodation ('000)

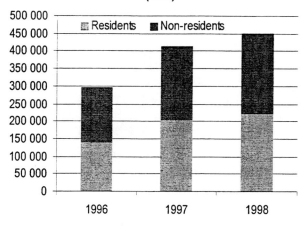

Key figures on tourism

Hotels and similar establishments

	1997	1998
Number of establishments	50	67
Number of bed-places	6 168	6 371
Average net rate of utilisation (%)	:	:

Nights spent in collective tourist accommodation (000s)

	1996	1997	1998
Total nights spent	296 225	414 782	452 763
Nights spent by residents	138 522	202 909	221 806
Nights spent by non-residents	157 703	211 873	230 957
of which: EU share (%)	:	:	:

Resident and non-resident shares of total nights spent in collective tourist accommodation - 2000

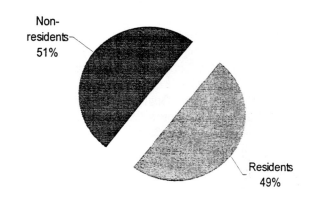

Hotels and similar establishments

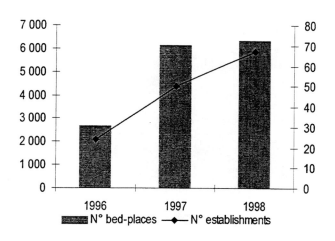

BULGARIA

Key statistics - 2000

Population	8 190 876
Surface area	110 993 km²
Population density (inhabitants/km²)	73.8
Increase in GDP	5.8%
Exchange rate 1 EURO = BGL	:
Increase of consumer price index	:
Increase of hotels, cafés and restaurants consumer price index	:

Recent trends

Data for 2000 indicate that the number of hotels and similar establishments reached 648 units recording a growth rate of 25.1% compared to 1999. The bed-places followed the same trend but at a lesser growth rate of +20.4%.

After declining in 1999, the total nights spent in collective accommodation establishments nearly reached the previous level of 1998. With over 8.5 million, nights rose by 34% compared to 1999. This result is mainly due to the rise of nights spent in hotels and similar establishments (+16.5%) since other collective accommodation establishments recorded a drop of 19%. Both resident (+8.6%) and non-resident (+18%) nights grew in 2000. EU 15 resident overnight stays rose by 12% and accounted for 71% of foreign tourist demand.

Arrivals of visitors at the borders continued to decline in 2000 at a lesser rate of -2.7% compared to -3.5% in 1999. Tourists represented 56.6% of 2000 visitors.
Bulgaria was a net earner of tourism services in 1998 with a positive result of EURO 193.2 million in terms of international trade.

In 1998, employment in the hotels and restaurants sector amounted to 75 800 persons.

Total nights spent in collective tourist accommodation ('000)

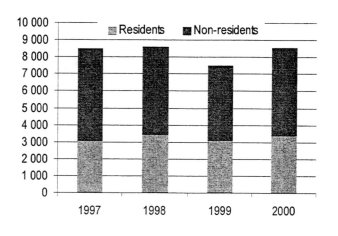

Key figures on tourism

Hotels and similar establishments

	1999	2000
Number of establishments	518	648
Number of bed-places	100 663	121 222
Average net rate of utilisation (%)	29.7	28.3

Nights spent in collective tourist accommodation (000s)

	1998	1999	2000
Total nights spent	8 635	6 389	8 554
Nights spent by residents	3 438	3 117	3 384
Nights spent by non-residents	5 197	4 382	5 170
of which: EU share (%)	59.2	74.7	70.9

Resident and non-resident shares of total nights spent in collective tourist accommodation - 2000

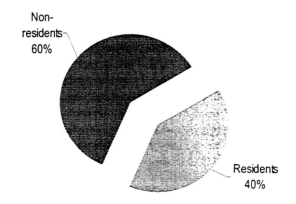

Arrivals at the borders ('000)

	1998	1999	2000
Visitors	5 240	5 056	4 922
Tourists	2 667	2 491	2 785

Balance of Payments - Travel (Mio EURO)

	1998	1999	2000
Credits	392	:	:
Debits	198	:	:
Balance	193	:	:

Arrivals at the borders ('000)

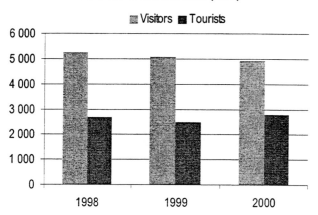

CROATIA

Key statistics* - 2000

Population[1]	4 554 000
Surface area	56 542 km²
Population density (inhabitants/km²)	80.54
Increase in GDP	3.7%
Exchange rate 1 EURO = HRK	7.63
Increase of consumer price index	5.3%
Increase of hotels, cafés and restaurants consumer price index	2.4%

*: data Central Bureau of Statistics Croatia, 1: 1999 data

Recent trends

2000 figures on the number of hotels and similar establishments reveal a growth rate of 6.1% indicating a continuation of the positive trend of the previous years. Bed-places grew by 3% in 2000 coming after a drop of nearly the same rate in 1999 compared to 1998. Total nights spent in collective tourist accommodation grew impressively by 37.3% in 2000 after a drop of 11.1% in 1999 compared to 1998.

A rise of 38.7% of the activity of the hotels and similar establishments combined with an increase of 35.5% of the nights spent in the other kinds of collective accommodation establishments explained the remarkable growth rate of total nights in 2000. Resident nights went down by 7.5% while non-resident overnight stays grew by 48.8%. 55.2% of foreign tourist demand is attributed to EU15 residents, whose number of overnight stays rose by 54.9%. In 2000, data on arrivals of visitors indicate a rise of 27.5% confirming the positive trend of 1999 and 1998. 2000 growth rate is however more important than those of the previous years. The travel item in the balance of payments showed a considerable surplus in 2000, which represented an increase of 44.1% after a drop of 13.5% in 1999. The 2000 result is attributable to the sharp fall in travel expenditures that declined by 11.7% combined with a rise of 22.3% of travel receipts. In 2000, employment in hotels and restaurants sector in Croatia amounted to 73,771 persons, recording an increase of 10.5% with respect to 1999.

Key figures on tourism

Hotels and similar establishments

	1999	2000
Number of establishments	691	733
Number of bed-places	193 716	199 474
Average net rate of utilisation (%)	:	:

Nights spent in collective tourist accommodation (000s)

	1998	1999	2000
Total nights spent	25 832	22 470	30 858
Nights spent by residents	4 495	4 568	4 224
Nights spent by non-residents	21 337	17 902	26 634
of which: EU share (%)	57.2	53.0	55.2

Resident and non-resident shares of total nights spent in

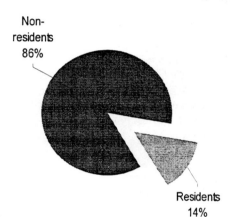

Non-residents 86%

Residents 14%

collective tourist accommodation - 2000

Arrivals at the borders ('000)

	1998	1999	2000
Visitors	24 379	28 211	35 961
Tourists	:	:	:

Balance of Payments - Travel (Mio EURO)

	1998	1999	2000
Credits	2 451	2 355	3 000
Debits	536	699	612
Balance	1 916	1 657	2 388

Total nights spent in collective tourist accommodation ('000)

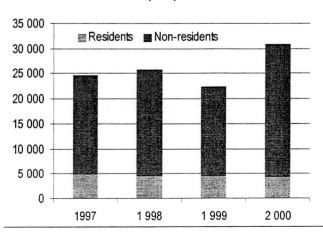

Travel item in the Balance of Payments (Mio EURO)

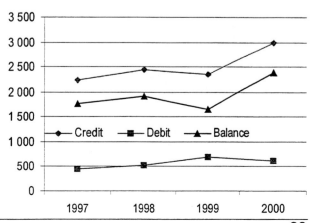

Key statistics - 2000

Population	10 278 098
Surface area	78 866 km²
Population density (inhabitants/km²)	130.3
Increase in GDP	2.9%
Exchange rate 1 EURO = CZK	35.5995
Increase of consumer price index	:
Increase of hotels, cafés and restaurants consumer price index	6.6%

Recent trends

The number of hotels and similar establishments rose by 2.1% in 2000. This rise came after a drop of -1.5% recorded in 1999. The bed-places kept growing (+3.8%) continuing the upward trend of the previous years.

With respect to 1999, total nights spent in collective accommodation grew by 7.8% in 2000. Resident overnight stays grew by 13.8%, while foreign tourists' demand decreased by 1.8%. EU15 residents' overnight stays rose by 2.5% in 2000 and represented 69% of non-resident demand. Nights spent in hotels and similar establishments grew by 11.7% while the demand recorded in other kinds of collective accommodation establishments increased by 3.4%.

Arrivals of visitors at the borders grew by 3.4% in 2000. This result came after a drop of 2% recorded in 1999 with respect of 1998.

The surplus of the travel item of the Balance of Payments grew by 19.3% in 2000. This result is explained by a rise of 9.2% of travel receipts combined with a drop of -1.5% of travel expenditures. Though at a lesser rate of -1.5% compared to -17.1% in 1999 and -20.6% in 1998, travel expenditures continued their downward trend in 2000.

Employment in hotels and restaurants sector grew by 1.7% in 2000 and amounted to 119,602 persons.

Total nights spent in collective tourist accommodation ('000)

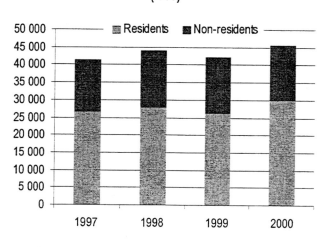

Key figures on tourism

Hotels and similar establishments

	1999	2000
Number of establishments	3 614	3 690
Number of bed-places	203 819	211 631
Average net rate of utilisation (%)	33.6	46.0

Nights spent in collective tourist accommodation (000s)

	1998	1999	2000
Total nights spent	44 054	42 349	45 661
Nights spent by residents	27 836	26 224	29 830
Nights spent by non-residents	16 218	16 125	15 831
of which: EU share (%)	64.0	66.1	69.0

Resident and non-resident shares of total nights spent in collective tourist accommodation - 2000

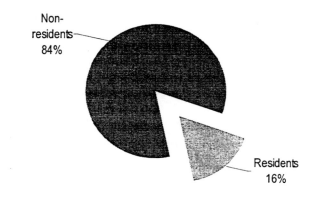

Arrivals at the borders ('000)

	1998	1999	2000
Visitors	102 844	100 832	104 247
Tourists	:	:	:

Balance of Payments - Travel (Mio EURO)

	1998	1999	2000
Credits	3 319	2 847	3 110
Debits	1 668	1 383	1 362
Balance	1 651	1 464	1 747

Travel item in the Balance of Payments (Mio EURO)

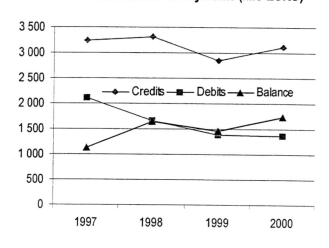

ESTONIA

Key statistics - 2000

Population	1 439 197
Surface area	45 227 km²
Population density (inhabitants/km²)	31.8
Increase in GDP	6.9%
Exchange rate 1 EURO = EEK	15.6466
Increase of consumer price index	:
Increase of hotels, cafés and restaurants consumer price index	5.7%

Recent trends

With a growth rate of 6.4%, the number of collective tourist accommodation establishments rose again in 2000. The number of bed-places followed the same trend with a growth rate of 1.6%. total nights spent in hotels and similar establishments grew up by 15.4% in 2000 confirming the upward trend of the previous years. The rise of total nights is mainly due to the increasing demand of foreign tourists. Non-resident nights spent grew by 19.9% in 2000 continuing the positive trend of the previous years. Resident nights spent also rose but at a lower rate of 4.6%. EU15 residents represented 82.4% of this foreign tourist demand, with a growth rate of 21% recorded in 2000 compared to 1999.

International visitor arrivals grew by 4.1% in 2000 compared to previous year. EU15 visitors arrivals rose by 2.3% and represented 68% of total inbound visitor flows. Arrivals of tourists grew significantly by 26.3% in 2000 compared to 1999.

In 2000, Estonia remained a net earner of tourism services. The surplus of the travel item in the balance of payment rose by 3.6% in 2000 after a drop of nearly 12% in 1999. Travel receipts as well as travel expenditures kept rising respectively by 5.9% and 9.6% in 2000.

Employment in the hotels and restaurants sector numbered 12,133 persons in 1999.

Total nights spent in hotels and similar establishments ('000)

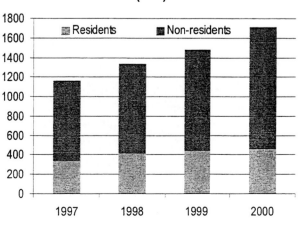

Key figures on tourism

Hotels and similar establishments

	1999	2000
Number of establishments	329	350
Number of bed-places	16 034	16 292
Average net rate of utilisation (%)	34.0	35.0

Nights spent in hotels and similar establishments (000s)

	1998	1999	2000
Total nights spent	1 339	1 484	1 712
Nights spent by residents	413	439	459
Nights spent by non-residents	926	1 045	1 253
of which: EU share (%)	78.9	81.6	82.4

Resident and non-resident shares of total nights spent in hotels and similar establishments – 2000

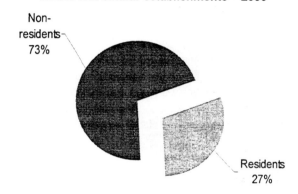

Arrivals at the borders ('000)

	1998	1999	2000
Visitors	2 909	3 181	3 310
Tourists	825	950	1 200

Balance of Payments - Travel (Mio EURO)

	1998	1999	2000
Credits	477	518	549
Debits	119	202	221
Balance	358	316	327

Travel item in the Balance of Payments (Mio EURO)

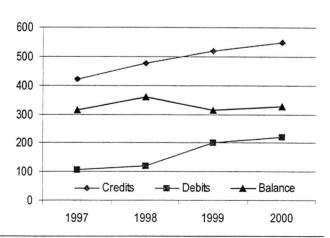

Key statistics - 2000

Population	:
Surface area	25 713 km²
Population density (inhabitants/km²)	
Increase in GDP	na%
Exchange rate 1 EURO = MKD	60.6935
Increase of consumer price index	:
Increase of hotels, cafés and restaurants consumer price index	5.8%

Recent trends

With a growth rate of 13.3%, a figure more than the triple of the rate of 1999, the number of hotels and similar establishments grew substantially in 2000. The bed-places went down by 2.9% interrupting the positive trend of the previous years and indicating a concentration of capacity.

Total nights spent in collective tourist accommodation establishments remained stable over the past three years. Despite a rise of 2.5% in total nights spent in hotels and similar establishments, 2000 result is attributable to a drop of 4.6% of the total nights spent in other kinds of collective accommodation establishments.

Resident nights declined by 1.6% while foreign tourist demand grew by 2.3%. EU15 resident overnight stays decreased by 23% and represented 27.3% of the foreign tourist demand.

The number of arrivals of tourists at the borders grew by 23.8% in 2000 continuing the positive trend of the previous years. Tourists represented 7.8% of total inbound visitor flows. In 2000, FYROM was a net earner of tourism services although the surplus decreased by half (-52.1%). This was due to a higher growth rate of +22.8% of travel expenditures compared to a rise of 8.6% of travel receipts. Hotels and restaurants sector employed 9,998 persons in 1999.

Total nights spent in collective tourist accommodation ('000)

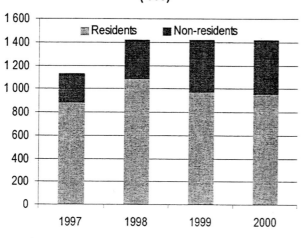

Key figures on tourism

Hotels and similar establishments

	1999	2000
Number of establishments	128	145
Number of bed-places	16 418	15 950
Average net rate of utilisation (%)	:	:

Nights spent in collective tourist accommodation (000s)

	1998	1999	2000
Total nights spent	1 420	1 424	1 420
Nights spent by residents	1 086	967	952
Nights spent by non-residents	334	457	468
of which: EU share (%)	22.9	36.3	27.3

Resident and non-resident shares of total nights spent in collective tourist accommodation - 2000

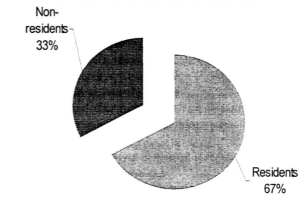

Arrivals at the borders ('000)

	1998	1999	2000
Visitors	1 848	2 223	2 865
Tourists	157	181	224

Balance of Payments - Travel (Mio EURO)

	1998	1999	2000
Credits	13	37	41
Debits	27	30	37
Balance	-13	7	4

Travel item in the Balance of Payments (Mio EURO)

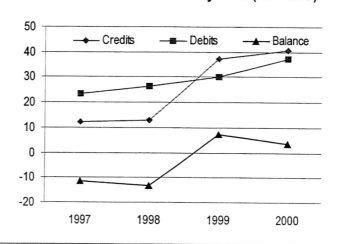

Key statistics - 2000

Population	10 043.224
Surface area	93 000 km²
Population density (inhabitants/km²)	108
Increase in GDP	5.2%
Exchange rate 1 EURO = HUF	260.045
Increase of consumer price index	:
Increase of hotels, cafés and restaurants consumer price index	:

Recent trends

Data for 2000 show a 4.2% increase in the number of hotels and similar establishments confirming the upward trend of the three previous years. The bed-places remained stable (0.7%) interrupting the positive trend of 1999 and 1998 and indicating a concentration of capacity.

Total nights spent in collective tourist accommodation grew by 13.5% in 2000 continuing the positive trend of the previous years. 2000 result was mainly due to a significant rise of 31% of the nights spent in the other kinds of collective accommodation establishments combined with an increase of 6.3% of the demand in hotels and similar establishments. Resident nights grew by 24.9% while non-resident overnight stays went up by 5.7%. In 2000, 70.3% of the nights spent by non-resident in Hungarian collective accommodation establishments was attributed to EU15 residents whose number of overnight stays grew by 10.6%.
Data on arrivals at the border indicate a rise of 8.1% of visitors. EU15 visitors declined by 6.7% in 2000.
Figures for 2000 indicate that Hungary remained a net earner of tourism services. Despite a rise of travel expenditures of 6.5%, travel receipts grew at a higher rate of 16.6%. The result was a growth rate of 22% of the travel surplus in the balance of payments.
In 2000, employment in hotels and catering sector remained stable (+0.1%) concerning 133,300 persons.

Total nights spent in collective tourist accommodation ('000)

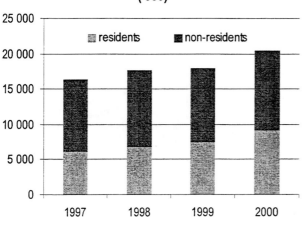

Key figures on tourism

Hotels and similar establishments

	1999	2000
Number of establishments	1 851	1 928
Number of bed-places	144 600	143 573
Average net rate of utilisation (%)	41.0	42.0

Nights spent in collective tourist accommodation (000s)

	1998	1999	2000
Total nights spent	17 650	17 993	20 430
Nights spent by residents	6 778	7 384	9 220
Nights spent by non-residents	10 872	10 609	11 210
of which: EU share (%)	:	67.1	70.3

Resident and non-resident shares of total nights spent in collective tourist accommodation 2000

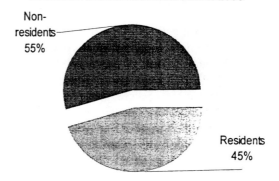

Non-residents 55%

Residents 45%

Arrivals at the borders ('000)

	1998	1999	2000
Visitors	33 624	28 803	31 141
Tourists	:	:	:

Balance of Payments - Travel (Mio EURO)

	1998	1999	2000
Credits	3 145	3 198	3 729
Debits	997	1 118	1 191
Balance	2 147	2 080	2 537

Travel item in the Balance of Payments (Mio EURO)

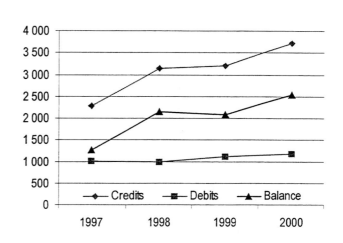

LATVIA

Key statistics - 2000

Population	2 424 150
Surface area	64 589 km²
Population density (inhabitants/km²)	37.5
Increase in GDP	6.6%
Exchange rate 1 EURO = LVL	0.559431
Increase of consumer price index	:
Increase of hotels, cafés and restaurants consumer price index	2.1%

Recent trends

The number of hotels and similar establishments grew by 10.7% in 2000 with 16 more establishments than in 1999. The decline of bed-places continued in 2000 but at a lesser rate of 4.5% compared to 8.5% in 1999.

Total nights spent in collective tourist accommodation rose by 3.5% in 2000 after a period of stability (-0.5%) in 1999. 2000 result is attributable to a rise of activity of 4.5% in hotels and similar establishments while the other kind of collective accommodation establishments recorded a drop of 6.8% of their nights spent. Resident nights grew by 10.9% and non-resident overnight stays went down by 3.7%. EU15 resident overnight stays remained stable (-0.3%) and represented 44.3% of foreign tourist demand.

In 2000, the arrivals of visitors at the borders grew by 8.3%. But with a negative rate of 8.5%, EU 15 visitors were less. Though travel receipts increased substantially by 25.3% and travel expenditures only rose by 4.4%, 2000 figures on the travel item in the balance of payments indicate a deficit confirming the negative trend of the previous years. In 2000, however the deficit decreased by 12%. Employment in hotels and restaurants sector remained stable in 2000 and amounted to 23,900 persons.

Total nights spent in collective tourist accommodation ('000)

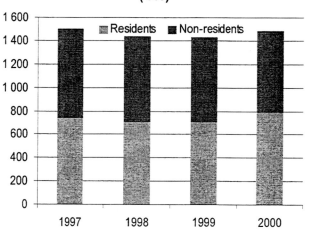

Key figures on tourism

Hotels and similar establishments

	1999	2000
Number of establishments	150	166
Number of bed-places	12 453	11 890
Average net rate of utilisation (%)	29.6	32.0

Nights spent in collective tourist accommodation (000s)

	1998	1999	2000
Total nights spent	1 441	1 434	1 484
Nights spent by residents	708	710	787
Nights spent by non-residents	733	724	697
of which: EU share (%)	39.2	42.7	44.3

Resident and non-resident shares of total nights spent in collective tourist accommodation - 2000

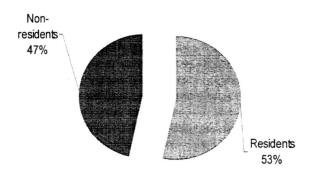

Arrivals at the borders ('000)

	1998	1999	2000
Visitors	1 788	1 738	1 882
Tourists	567	489	452

Balance of Payments - Travel (Mio EURO)

	1998	1999	2000
Credits	163	114	142
Debits	273	258	270
Balance	-110	-145	-128

Travel item in the Balance of Payments (Mio EURO)

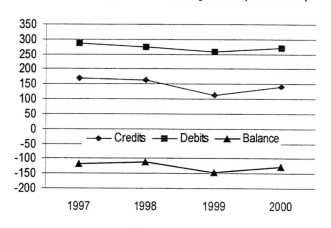

LITHUANIA

Key statistics - 2000

Population	3 698 521
Surface area	65 300
Population density (inhabitants/km²)	56.6
Increase in GDP	3.3%
Exchange rate 1 EURO = LTL	3.69454
Increase of consumer price index	:
Increase of hotels, cafés and restaurants consumer price index	0%

Recent trends

Data for 2000 show a small increase of 2.7% in the number of hotels and similar establishments indicating an expansion of tourism supply. Nevertheless in terms of bed-places capacity after having amounted to 11,714 in 1998, it has been declining.

In 2000 the total nights spent in collective accommodation went down by 18.7%. This result is attributable to a drop of 31.8% of total nights spent in the other kinds of collective accommodation establishments. Nights spent in hotels and similar establishments also declined, but at a more moderate rate of 4.1%. The drop of the total nights is also the result of the decline of both resident (-27.2%) and foreign (-2.7%) demand. Overnight stays by EU15 residents grew by 1.7% and represented 45.8% of foreign tourist demand. The arrivals of visitors at the borders decreased by 8.1% interrupting the positive trend of the previous years. Nevertheless in 2000, only 26.5% of the visitors were tourists. EU15 visitors grew by 19.5% in 2000.

In 2000, despite a decline of 23.8% of the travel surplus, Lithuania was still a net earner of tourism services. The travel receipts as well as the travel expenditures went down respectively by 17.9% and 14.3%.

Employment in tourism sector grew by 4.9% in 2000 and involved 28,000 persons.

Total nights spent in collective tourist accommodation ('000)

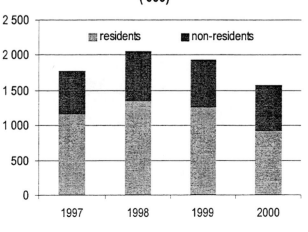

Key figures on tourism

Hotels and similar establishments

	1999	2000
Number of establishments	221	227
Number of bed-places	11 553	11 489
Average net rate of utilisation (%)	24.6	22.8

Nights spent in collective tourist accommodation (000s)

	1998	1999	2000
Total nights spent	2 061	1 936	1 575
Nights spent by residents	1 348	1 261	919
Nights spent by non-residents	713	675	657
of which: EU share (%)	42.7	43.8	45.8

Resident and non-resident shares of total nights spent in collective tourist accommodation - 2000

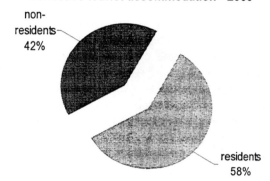

non-residents 42%

residents 58%

Arrivals at the borders ('000)

	1998	1999	2000
Visitors	4 287	4 454	4 092
Tourists	1 416	1 422	1 083

Balance of Payments - Travel (Mio EURO)

	1998	1999	2000
Credits	409	516	423
Debits	260	319	274
Balance	149	196	150

Travel item in the Balance of Payments (Mio EURO)

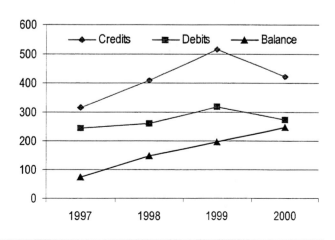

POLAND

Key statistics - 2000

Population	38 644 211
Surface area	31 268 km²
Population density (inhabitants/km²)	1 236
Increase in GDP	4.0%
Exchange rate 1 EURO = PLN	4.00817
Increase of consumer price index	10.1%
Increase of hotels, cafés and restaurants consumer price index *	8.1%

Recent trends

After considerable expansion in 1998, the number of hotels and similar establishments declined by 5.6% in 2000 compared to 1999, continuing the downward trend of the previous year. The number of bed-places remained stable (0.0%) in 2000.

The total nights spent in collective accommodation establishments grew by 5.9% in 2000. Resident overnight stays accounted for 86% of total nights spent. In 2000, resident nights grew by 3.6% after declining by 17.5% in 1999. Hotels and similar establishments recorded 22% of resident overnight stays in collective tourist accommodation as a whole in 2000.

Non-resident nights spent grew significantly by 22.1% in 2000 following a drop of 23% recorded in 1999. 72% of the foreign tourist nights spent were recorded in hotels and similar establishments.

Overnight stays in hotels and similar establishments grew by 22.7% in 2000 interrupting the downward trend of the previous years. Nights spent in other kinds of collective accommodation establishments remained stable (+0.1%) in 2000 following a drop of 15.7% in 1999.

Figures on arrivals of visitors at the borders showed stability (+0.6%) in 1999.

Total nights spent in collective tourist accommodation ('000)

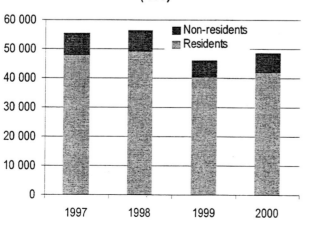

Key figures on tourism

Hotels and similar establishments

	1999	2000
Number of establishments	1 535	1 449
Number of bed-places	120 285	120 280
Average net rate of utilisation (%)	38.6	35.1

Nights spent in collective tourist accommodation (000s)

	1998	1999	2000
Total nights spent	56 344	46 096	48 794
Nights spent by residents	49 011	40 451	41 903
Nights spent by non-residents	7 333	5 645	6 891
of which: EU share (%)	:	:	:

Resident and non-resident shares of total nights spent in collective tourist accommodation - 2000

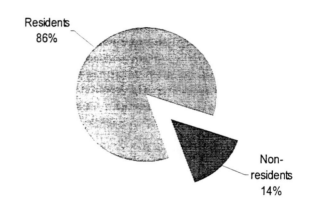

Arrivals at the borders ('000)

	1998	1999	2000
Visitors	88 592	89 118	:
Tourists	:	:	:

Hotels and similar establishments

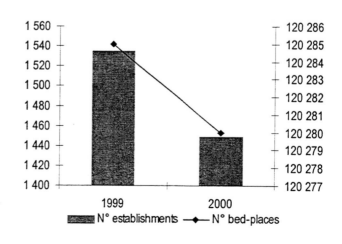

R O M A N I A

Key statistics - 2000

Population	22 455 485
Surface area	238 391 km²
Population density (inhabitants/km²)	94.2
Increase in GDP	1.6%
Exchange rate 1 EURO = ROL	19921.8
Increase of consumer price index	-0.1%
Increase of hotels, cafés and restaurants consumer price index	-4.0%

Recent trends

2000 data on the numbers of hotels and similar establishments indicate a drop of 4.8% breaking the positive trend of the previous years. The bed-places also went down in 2000 but at a lesser rate of 1.7%.

In 2000, the total number spent in collective accommodation establishments remained stable (-0.1%) interrupting the negative trend of the previous years. This result is mainly explained by the stability (+0.3%) of the nights spent in hotels and similar establishments since the demand recorded in the other kinds of collective accommodation went down by 3.8%.

Resident nights decreased by 1.2% while foreign tourist demand grew significantly by 8.6%. EU 15 resident overnight stays grew by 11.1% and accounted for 56% of foreign tourist demand.

Arrivals of visitors at the borders remained stable (+0.8%) in 2000 after recording a significant growth of 8.1% in 1999.

The deficit of the travel item of the Balance of Payment was reduced in 2000 by 56.1% confirming the positive trend of 1999. 2000 result is due to a significant growth of travel receipts (+35.4%) combined with a moderate rise (2.3%) of travel expenditures.
The tourism sector employed 100,000 persons in 1999.

Key figures on tourism

Hotels and similar establishments

	1999	2000
Number of establishments	2 660	2 533
Number of bed-places	202 867	199 333
Average net rate of utilisation (%)	37.1	38.4

Nights spent in collective tourist accommodation (000s)

	1998	1999	2000
Total nights spent	19 183	17 670	17 647
Nights spent by residents	16 977	15 690	15 497
Nights spent by non-residents	2 206	1 980	2 149
of which: EU share (%)	52.8	54.7	56.0

Resident and non-resident shares of total nights spent in collective tourist accommodation - 2000

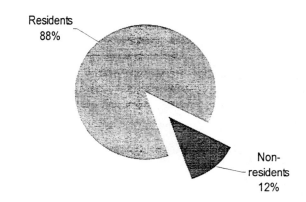

Residents 88%

Non-residents 12%

Arrivals at the borders ('000)

	1998	1999	2000
Visitors	4 831	5 224	5 264
Tourists	:	:	:

Balance of Payments - Travel (Mio EURO)

	1998	1999	2000
Credits	232	236	320
Debits	409	371	379
Balance	-177	-134	-59

Total nights spent in collective tourist accommodation ('000)

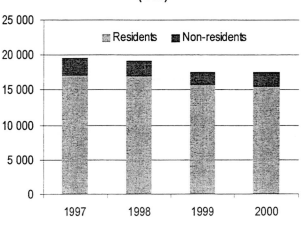

Travel item in the Balance of Payments (Mio EURO)

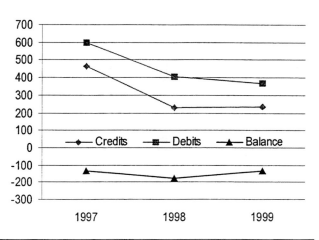

SLOVAKIA

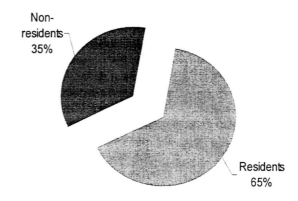

Key statistics - 2000

Population	5 398 657
Surface area	49 035 km²
Population density (inhabitants/km²)	110
Increase in GDP	2.2%
Exchange rate 1 EURO = SKK	42.4840
Increase of consumer price index	:
Increase of hotels, cafés and restaurants consumer price index	:

Recent trends

With twelve more units, the number of hotels and similar establishments kept growing in 2000 but at a lesser rate of 2.1% compared to 5% in 1999. The bed-places followed the same pattern with a positive growth rate of 1.7% in 2000 in retreat compared to 2.7% recorded in 1999.

In 2000, the total nights spent in collective accommodation establishments decreased by 3.7% breaking the positive trend of the two previous years. This result is mostly due to the drop of 8.4% of domestic tourism which was more accentuated in other kinds of collective accommodation establishment (-10.6%) compared to the drop recorded in hotels and similar establishments (-5.1%). Foreign tourist demand continued to grow in 2000 but at a lower rate of 6.3% compared to 7% in 1999. Overnight stays by EU15 residents grew by 9% and represented 34.6% of foreign tourist demand.

Figures on arrivals of visitors at the borders saw a drop of 6.5% in 2000. Arrivals fell by 6% in 1999 after a rise of 3.1% in 1998.

The surplus of the travel item in the Balance of Payments grew by 29.9% in 2000 indicating a continuation of the trend of the previous years. 2000 result is due to a rise of 8.3% of the travel receipts while tourism expenditures remained stable (+0.5%).

Total nights spent in collective tourist accommodation ('000)

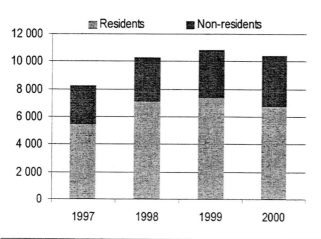

Key figures on tourism

Hotels and similar establishments

	1999	2000
Number of establishments	570	582
Number of bed-places	50 199	51 040
Average net rate of utilisation (%)	31.9	31.7

Nights spent in collective tourist accommodation (000s)

	1998	1999	2000
Total nights spent	10 329	10 863	10 464
Nights spent by residents	7 073	7 379	6 760
Nights spent by non-residents	3 256	3 484	3 704
of which: EU share (%)	36.2	33.8	34.6

Resident and non-resident shares of total nights spent in collective tourist accommodation - 2000

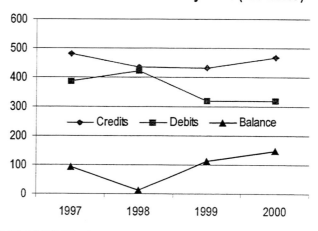

Arrivals at the borders ('000)

	1998	1999	2000
Visitors	32 735	30 757	28 769
Tourists	:	:	:

Balance of Payments - Travel (Mio EURO)

	1998	1999	2000
Credits	436	432	468
Debits	423	319	320
Balance	13	114	149

Travel item in the Balance of Payments (Mio EURO)

SLOVENIA

Key statistics - 2000

Population	1 987 755
Surface area	20 273 km²
Population density (inhabitants/km²)	98
Increase in GDP	4.6%
Exchange rate 1 EURO = SIT	206.613
Increase of consumer price index	:
Increase of hotels, cafés and restaurants consumer price index	5.1%

Recent trends

2000 data on the number of hotels and similar establishments indicate a 12.6% growth, breaking the declining trend of 1999 and 1998. Data on bed-places follow a similar pattern with a rise of 3.5% in 2000 after a decline of 3.7% in 1999.

Total nights spent in collective accommodation rose by 10.9% in 2000 after a drop of 3.7% in 1999. This result is attributable to a rise of nights spent both in hotels and similar establishments (+12.1%) and in the other kinds of collective accommodation establishments (+8.1%). Resident nights remained stable (-0.3%) while non-resident overnight stays rose significantly by 24.7%.

EU15 resident nights grew by 27.6% and accounted for 71.7% of foreign tourist demand. The number of arrival of visitors at the borders went up by 6% in 2000 breaking the slump in 1999. 34.3% of the visitors were tourists in 2000. The surplus of travel item in the balance of payments, which was declining the previous years, grew by 22.3% in 2000. With a rate of 15.7%, travel receipts followed the same pattern interrupting the declining trend of the previous years.

The travel expenditures kept rising in 2000 but at a lesser rate of 10.6%. In 2000, employment in hotels and restaurants sector in Slovenia amounted to 28,899 persons, recording an increase of 3% with respect to 1999.

Key figures on tourism

Hotels and similar establishments

	1999	2000
Number of establishments	398	448
Number of bed-places	29 541	30 576
Average net rate of utilisation (%)	36.6	39.4

Nights spent in collective tourist accommodation (000s)

	1998	1999	2000
Total nights spent	6 095	5 870	6 509
Nights spent by residents	3 161	3 243	3 232
Nights spent by non-residents	2 934	2 627	3 277
of which: EU share (%)	72.4	70.1	71.7

Resident and non-resident shares of total nights spent in collective tourist accommodation - 2000

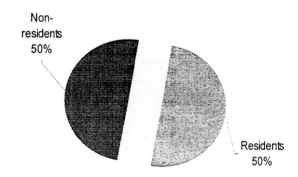

Non-residents 50%

Residents 50%

Arrivals at the borders ('000)

	1998	1999	2000
Visitors	3 297	3 000	3 179
Tourists	977	884	1 090

Balance of Payments - Travel (Mio EURO)

	1998	1999	2000
Credits	972	891	1 031
Debits	499	504	557
Balance	474	388	474

Travel item in the Balance of Payments (Mio EURO)

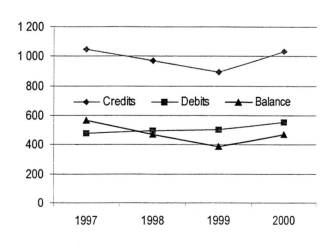

Total nights spent in collective tourist accommodation ('000)

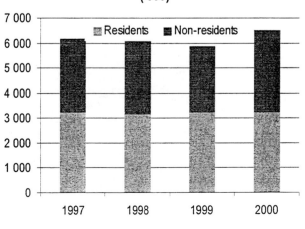

Key statistics - 2000

Population	30 170 000
Surface area	2 381 740km²
Population density (inhabitants/km²)	12.6
Increase in GDP	2.4%
Exchange rate 1 EURO = DZD	75.26
Increase of consumer price index	0.3%
Increase of hotels, cafés and restaurants consumer price index	:

Recent trends

In 2000 the number of hotels and similar establishments increased by 2.6%, with 21 more establishments than in 1999. The corresponding capacity in terms of bed-places increased by 1%, with 700 additional bed-places.

In 2000 the total number of nights spent in hotels and similar establishments increased by 11.8% compared to the previous year, amounting to 3.8 million. Nights spent by non-residents increased by almost 20.8% and nights spent by EU guests increased by 15.5%. EU citizens represented 52% of nights spent by non-residents in 2000.

The total number of international visitor arrivals increased by nearly 16% in 2000 compared to 1999. Arrivals of EU visitors increased by 35%. Nationals residing abroad still make up the largest share of total arrivals (61%). The share of visitor arrivals of EU citizens, represented nearly 11% in 2000, compared to 9% in 1999. France, Italy and Germany are the main EU generating markets.

Foreign trade receipts in tourism represented 11% of total services receipts in 1999, but only 0.6% of current account receipts. In 2000 international travel receipts increased by 38%, while expenditures fell by 11%; and so the deficit of the travel account decreased by a third. Employment in hotels and catering in the public sector totalled 13,524 jobs in 2000, increasing by 12% compared to 1999.

Total nights spent in hotels and similar establishments (000's)

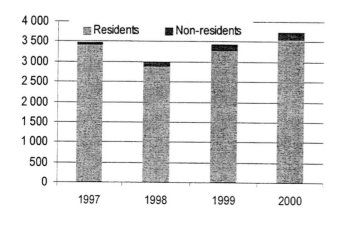

Key figures on tourism

Hotels and similar establishments

	1999	2000
Number of establishments	800	821
Number of bed-places	71 300	72 000
Average net rate of utilisation (%)	38.0	40.1

Nights spent in hotels and similar establishments (000s)

	1998	1999	2000
Total nights spent	3 003	3 439	3 845
Nights spent by residents	2 870	3 275	3 545
Nights spent by non-residents	133	164	198
of which: EU share (%)	59.2	54.0	51.7

Resident and non-resident shares of total nights spent in hotels and similar establishments - 2000

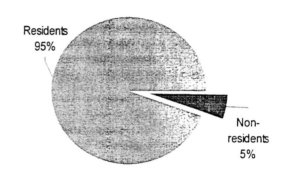

Arrivals at the borders ('000)

	1998	1999	2000
Visitors	678	749	866
Tourists	:	:	:

Balance of Payments - Travel (Mio EURO)

	1998	1999	2000
Credits	66	75	104
Debits	240	235	209
Balance	-174	-160	105

Travel item in the Balance of Payments (Mio EURO)

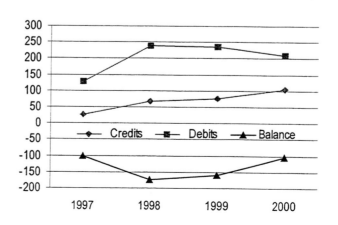

Population	759 000
Surface area	9 251km²
Population density (inhabitants/km²)	82
Increase in GDP*	4.8%
Exchange rate 1 EURO = CYP	0.53
Increase of consumer price index	4.3%
Increase of hotels, cafés and restaurants consumer price index	:

* estimate

Recent trends

In 2000 the number of hotels and similar establishments remained stable (0.5%), with a 1.4% increase in the number of bed-places on offer.

The number of nights spent by non-residents in hotels and similar establishments peaked in 1998, amounting to 14.4 million (10% compared to 1997).

In 2000 the number of arrivals of foreign tourists at the borders attained new heights, peaking at nearly 2.7 million, increasing by 10.3% compared to 1999. The number of tourists from the EU increased by 12.6% and accounted for nearly 80% of all tourist arrivals. The UK represents the largest influx of foreign tourists accounting for over 1.3 million arrivals (+ 17.9% compared to 1999).

Tourism represents an important sector of the economy. An indication of its contribution to employment are the 25,900 employees in the hotel and catering sector (+3.6% compared to 1999). Although Cyprus's overall foreign trade account is negative, it enjoys a surplus foreign trade balance for tourism.

Travel receipts represented 40% of total foreign trade earnings and 58% of total international receipts in services. In 2000 travel receipts increased by 27.5% compared to 1999, and the surplus by 29.6%.

Key figures on tourism

Hotels and similar establishments

	1999	2000
Number of establishments	580	583
Number of bed-places	83 347	84 479
Average net rate of utilisation (%)	:	:

Nights spent in Hotels and similar establishments (000s)

	1998	1999	2000
Total nights spent	15 000	:	:
Nights spent by residents	570	:	:
Nights spent by non-residents	14 430	:	:
of which: EU share (%)	:	:	:

Arrivals at the borders ('000)

	1998	1999	2000
Visitors	2 357	2 578	:
Tourists	2 223	2 434	2 686

% share of arrivals of tourists at the borders – 2000

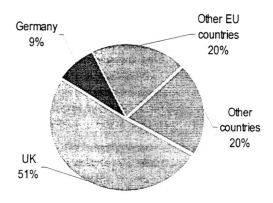

Balance of Payments - Travel (Mio EURO)

	1998	1999	2000
Credits	1 538	1 785	2 275
Debits	366	404	485
Balance	1 172	1 381	1 790

Arrivals of tourists at the borders (000's)

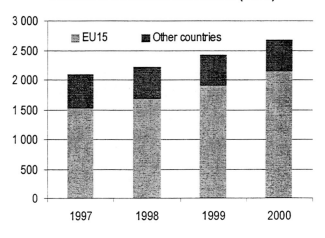

Travel item in the Balance of Payments (Mio EURO)

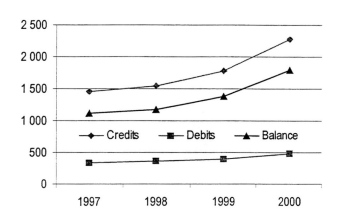

EGYPT

Key statistics - 2000

Population	63 309 000
Surface area	1 001 450km²
Population density (inhabitants/km²)	63.2
Increase in GDP	:
Exchange rate 1 EURO = EGP	3.20
Increase of consumer price index	2.7%
Increase of hotels, cafés and restaurants consumer price index	:

Recent trends

In 2000 there were 96 more hotels and similar establishments (+ 10.5%) amounting to 39 938 more bed-places (+21.3%) than in 1999.

Egypt quickly recovered from the slump in inbound tourism of 1998. The number of nights spent by non-residents in hotels and similar establishments amounted to over 31 million in 1999 and nearly 33 million in 2000, increasing in 2000 by 5.8% over the previous year. Nights spent by EU residents increased by 10.5% in 2000.

These positive results were also largely reflected in the number of arrivals of foreign visitors, with arrivals in 1999 reaching the unprecedented figure of nearly 4.8 million, and then again peaking in 2000 at over 5.5 million. Total foreign visitor arrivals increased by nearly 15% in 2000 compared to the previous year and arrivals of EU citizens increased by 24%. In 2000 the share of EU visitors accounted for 54% of total arrivals, compared to 50% in 1999.

Tourism makes a substantial contribution to Egypt's economy. In terms of foreign trade, travel receipts in 2000 accounted for 19% of total foreign trade earnings and 37% of total receipts in services. Travel receipts increased by 29% in 2000, and the surplus by 34%.

Nights spent by non-residents in hotels and similar establishments[1] ('000)

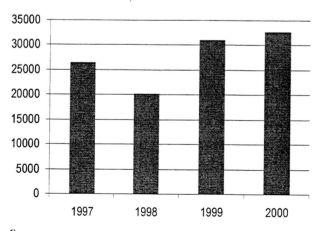

[1] Ministry of tourism classified accommodation

Key figures on tourism

Hotels and similar establishments[1]

	1999	2000
Number of establishments	914	1 010
Number of bed-places	187 284	227 222
Average net rate of utilisation (%)	67	73

Nights spent in hotels and similar establishments[1]

in (000s)	1998	1999	2000
Total nights spent	:	:	:
Nights spent by residents	:	:	:
Nights spent by non-residents	20 151	31 002	32 788
of which: EU share (%)	43.6	58.4	61.0

Nights spent by non-residents in hotels and similar establishments[1] - 2000

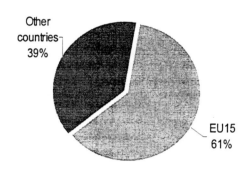

Arrivals at the borders ('000)

	1998	1999	2000
Visitors	4 941	6 995	:
Foreign visitors	3 454	4 797	5 506

Balance of Payments - Travel (Mio EURO)

	1998	1999	2000
Credits	2 287	3 662	4 713
Debits	1 028	1 011	1 164
Balance	1 259	2 651	3 549

Travel item in the Balance of Payments (Mio EURO)

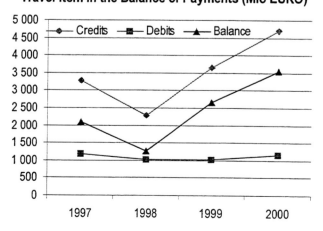

ISRAEL

eurostat

Key statistics - 2000

Population	6 364 000
Surface area	22 145 km²
Population density (inhabitants/km²)	287.4
Increase in GDP	6.0%
Exchange rate 1 EURO = ILS	3.76
Increase of consumer price index	1.1%
Increase of hotels, cafés and restaurants consumer price index	2.2%

Recent trends

In 2000 there were 10 more tourist hotels (+ 3.0%) amounting to 8,459 more bed-places (+8.6%) than in 1999.

Total nights spent in tourist hotels in 2000 increased by 5%, amounting to over 19.5 million. Domestic demand represented just over 50% of total nights spent and rose by 2% in 2000 (nearly 9.9 million). Nights spent by non-residents in tourist hotels amounted to nearly 9.7 million rising by 7% compared to the previous year. The share of nights spent by residents from European countries accounted for 55.6% in 2000 compared to 56.5% in 1999. The trend in non-resident nights was confirmed by a 4.5% increase in the total number of tourist arrivals at the borders, peaking at over 2.4 million in 2000, compared to 2.3 million in 1999. The share of arrivals from European countries accounted for 57.5% of total tourist arrivals, of which a very large proportion is made up of arrivals from EU countries (80%).

Tourism plays an important role in the economy. Accommodation services and restaurants employed 101,700 persons in 2000 (+12.7% compared to 1999), of which 86% were employees. The revised data series indicate a positive tourism foreign trade balance. Travel receipts grew by 24.2% in 2000 compared to 1999 and the surplus increased by 18.5%. In 2000 international travel receipts represented 7% of foreign trade earnings and 27% of total services receipts.

Total nights spent in Tourist hotels[1] ('000)

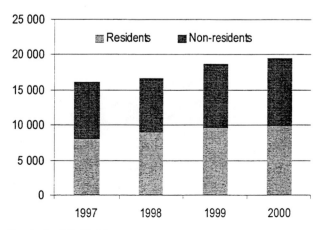

1) and not yet listed hotels

Key figures on tourism

Tourists hotels[1]

	1999	2000
Number of establishments	330	340
Number of bed-places	98 323	106 782
Average net rate of utilisation (%)	54.3	52.8

Nights spent in Tourist hotels[1] (000s)

	1998	1999	2000
Total nights spent	16 688	18 682	19 547
Nights spent by residents	8 978	9 635	9 870
Nights spent by non-residents	7 709	9 047	9 676
of which from Europe (%)	55.7	56.5	55.6

Resident and non-resident shares of total nights spent in Tourist hotels[1] - 2000

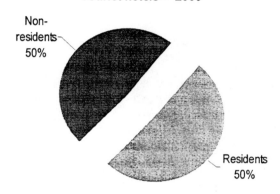

Arrivals at the borders ('000)

	1998	1999	2000
Visitors	2 200	2 566	2 672
Tourists	1 942	2 312	2 417

Balance of Payments - Travel (Mio EURO)

	1998	1999	2000
Credits	2 461	3 336	4 142
Debits	2 206	2 407	3 041
Balance	255	929	1 101

Travel item in the Balance of Payments (Mio EURO)

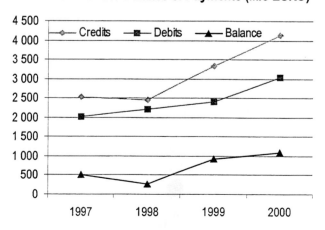

JORDAN

Key statistics - 2000

Population	5 039 000
Surface area	89 342 km²
Population density (inhabitants/km²)	56.4
Increase in GDP	3.9%
Exchange rate 1 ECU = JOD	0.6545
Increase of consumer price index	0.7%
Increase of hotels, cafés and restaurants consumer price index	:

Recent trends

In 2000 there were 30 more hotel and similar establishments than in 1999 (+7%), amounting to 2,668 bed-places (+8%).

Total nights spent in hotels and similar establishments grew by 2.7% compared to 1999, to reach 3.8 million in 2000. This was driven by a 4.3% increase in nights spent by non-residents, whereas resident nights fell by 6.2%.

In 2000 the number of arrivals of international visitors dropped by 9% compared to 1999, mainly attributable to the 12% drop in visitors from the Middle East, who represented 73% of total visitor arrivals. Arrivals of European visitors accounted for 17% of the total, but represented 23% of all tourist arrivals. The total number of tourist arrivals has experienced year to year increases, amounting to 1.4 million in 2000, increasing by 5% compared to the previous year.

Whereas, Jordan's overall foreign trade balance is negative, it enjoys a surplus in its travel account. Over the past years travel receipts have been rising significantly. In 2000 tourism foreign trade earnings increased by 5% compared to 1999. In 1999, travel receipts represented 11% of total foreign trade earnings and 18% of total receipts in services. Direct employment in the tourism industry accounted for 21,515 jobs in 2000, increasing by 4.6% compared to the previous year.

Total nights spent in hotels and similar establishments ('000)

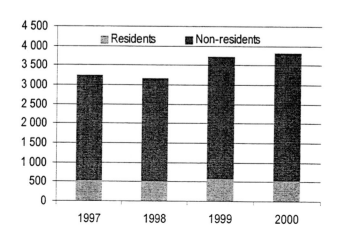

Key figures on tourism

Hotels and similar establishments

	1999	2000
Number of establishments	422	452
Number of bed-places	31 765	34 433
Average net rate of utilisation (%)	30.6	33.4

Nights spent in Hotels and similar establishments (000s)

	1998	1999	2000
Total nights spent	3 180	3 731	3 832
Nights spent by residents	498	577	541
Nights spent by non-residents	3 180	3 154	3 291
of which: EU share (%)	:	:	36.5

Resident and non-resident shares of total nights spent in hotels and similar establishments - 2000

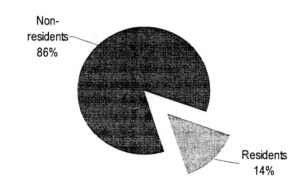

Arrivals at the borders ('000)

	1998	1999	2000
Visitors	3 303	3 315	3 019
Tourists	1 256	1 358	1 427

Balance of Payments - Travel (Mio EURO)

	1998	1999	2000
Credits	690	745	783
Debits	315	333	419
Balance	375	412	364

Travel item in the Balance of Payments (Mio EURO)

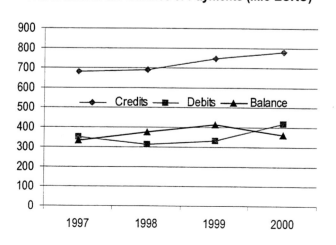

LEBANON

Key statistics - 2000

Population*	4 005 000
Surface area	10 400 km²
Population density (inhabitants/km²)	385.1
Increase in GDP	0.7%
Exchange rate 1 ECU = LBP	1 389.82
Increase of consumer price index*	0.7%
Increase of hotels, cafés and restaurants consumer price index	:

*1999

Recent trends

In 2000 there were 18 more hotels (+ 8.3%) amounting to 1,666 more bed-places (+8.4%) than in 1999.

Nights spent in hotels have been rising substantially over the past years; indeed doubling since 1997. In 2000, the number of nights totalled 297 000, 26.1% more than in 1999. Tourists from Europe represent 36% of total nights spent by non-residents.

Arrivals of visitors from abroad have confirmed this positive trend. In 2000 arrivals increased by 10.2%, amounting to 742 thousand, compared to nearly 673 thousand in 1999. Inbound tourism from European countries increased by 2.3%, and of which arrivals of EU citizens increased by nearly 6.7%. Arrivals from all European countries accounted for 31% of the total in 2000. Visitors from Arab countries represented 41% of the total arrivals from aboard. The main EU generating countries are France, Germany and the UK, accounting for respectively 9%, 5% and 3% of total visitor arrivals to Lebanon in 2000.

Tourism is destined to play an important role in the Lebanese economy. It is estimated that over 40 thousand persons were employed in the tourism sector in 2000, representing approximately 3% of total employment.

International tourism receipts have been rising over the past years rising, increasing by 24% in 2000 compared to 1999.

Total nights spent by non-residents in hotels ('000)

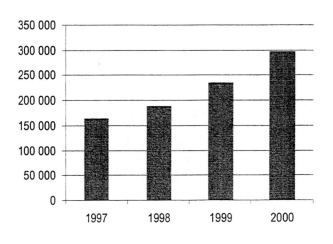

Key figures on tourism

Hotels

	1999	2000
Number of establishments	217	235
Number of bed-places	19 922	21 588
Average net rate of utilisation (%)	46.9	47.9

Nights spent in hotels (000s)

	1998	1999	2000
Total nights spent	:	:	:
Nights spent by residents	:	:	:
Nights spent by non-residents	189	236	297
of which: EU share (%)	27.3	24.2	25.6

Distribution of nights spent by non-residents in hotels - 2000

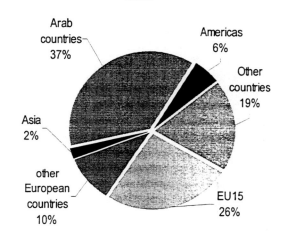

Arrivals at the borders ('000)

	1998	1999	2000
Visitors	631	673	742
Tourists	:	:	:

Balance of Payments - Travel (Mio EURO)

	1998	1999	2000
Credits	974	1 161	1 449
Debits	:	:	:
Balance	:	:	:

Balance of Payments - Travel credits (Mio EURO)

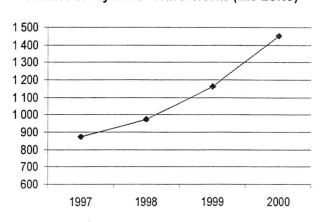

MALTA

Key statistics - 2000

Population	391 000
Surface area	316 km²
Population density (inhabitants/km²)	1 237
Increase in GDP*	5.5%
Exchange rate 1 ECU = mtl	0.40
Increase of consumer price index	2.4%
Increase of hotels, cafés and restaurants consumer price index	:

provisional

Recent trends

In 2000 there were 14 less hotels and similar establishments (-5.8%) amounting to 459 less bed-places (-1.1%) than in 1999.

The number of days spent by foreign tourists in hotels and similar establishments decreased by 14%, amounting to just over 7.9 million compared to nearly 9.2 million in 1999. Days spent in hotels and similar establishments accounted for 77% of the total days spent by inbound tourists, which amounted in total to 10.3 million in 2000 compared to 11.6 million in 1999 (-12%).

Total international tourist arrivals peaked at over 1.2 million in 1999, and remained at that level in 2000. Malta is a popular European holiday destination, with European tourists accounting for 91% of total arrivals from abroad in 2000. The UK and Germany are the main generating markets accounting for 35% and 17% of total tourist arrivals respectively.

Tourism makes an essential contribution to the Maltese economy. International travel receipts accounted for 13% of total foreign trade earnings and 55% of total receipts in services in 1999. Malta enjoys a tourism foreign trade surplus. In terms of employment the hotel and catering sector numbered 9,659 persons employed in 2000, representing 7% of total employment.

Total nights[1] spent by non-residents in hotels and similar establishments ('000)

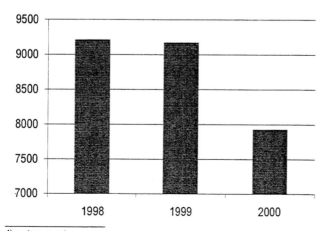

[1] = days spent

Key figures on tourism

Hotels and similar establishments

	1999	2000
Number of establishments	243	229
Number of bed-places	40 771	40 312
Gross rate of utilisation (%)	58.9	49.9

Nights[1] spent in Hotels and similar establishments ('000)

	1998	1999	2000
Total nights spent	:	:	:
Nights spent by residents	:	:	:
Nights spent by non-residents	9 215	9 173	7 927
of which: EU share (%)	81.5	86.5	84.9

EU share of total nights[1] spent by non-residents in hotels and similar establishments - 2000

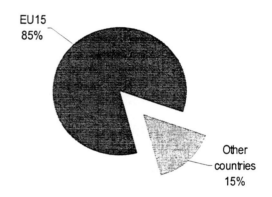

Arrivals at the borders ('000)

	1998	1999	2000
Visitors	1 198	1 229	1 240
Tourists	1 182	1 214	1 216

Balance of Payments - Travel (Mio EURO)

	1998	1999	2000
Credits	585	637	664
Debits	172	188	217
Balance	413	449	447

Travel item in the Balance of Payments (Mio EURO)

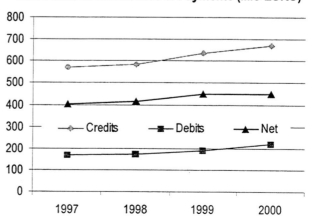

MOROCCO

Key statistics - 2000

Population	28 705 000
Surface area	710 850 km²
Population density (inhabitants/km²)	40.4
Increase in GDP	0.3%
Exchange rate 1 EURO = MAD	9.80
Increase of consumer price index	1.9%
Increase of hotels, cafés and restaurants consumer price index	:

Recent trends

Tourist accommodation supply remained fairly stable in the year 2000, with 3 more hotels and similar establishments on offer than in 1999, amounting to 856 more bed-places.

In 2000 the total number of nights spent in hotels and similar establishments increased by 3.4%, amounting to the unprecedented figure of over 16.5 million. Nights spent by residents and non-residents increased at the same pace (3.6% and 3.0% respectively). Nights spent by EU tourists represented 81% of non-resident nights.

Figures for total tourist arrivals at the borders reached new heights in 2000, amounting to over 4.1 million and increasing by 7.8% compared to 1999. Arrivals of EU tourists accounted for 50% of total tourist arrivals in 2000, and increased in number by 9.5% compared to 1999. Nationals residing abroad represent a large proportion of tourist arrivals to Morocco (40% in 2000).

Tourism makes an essential contribution to Morocco's economy. Direct and indirect employment in the tourism sector amounted to 628 000 jobs in 2000, increasing by 1.3% compared to 1999. In terms of the foreign trade receipts the travel account represents 15% of total foreign trade earnings and 68% of total receipts in services in 2000. International travel receipts reached new heights increasing by 21% compared to 1999. Morocco enjoys a substantial surplus travel account, which increased by 24% in 2000 compared to 1999.

Total nights spent in hotels and similar establishments ('000)

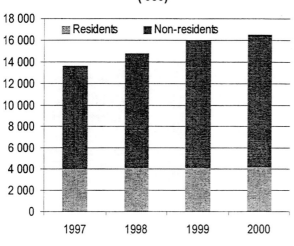

Key figures on tourism

Hotels and similar establishments

	1999	2000
Number of establishments	1 717	1 720
Number of bed-places	127 501	128 357
Average net rate of utilisation (%)	44.1	44.5

Nights spent in hotels and similar establishments (000s)

	1998	1999	2000
Total nights spent	14 790	15 979	16 524
Nights spent by residents	4 114	4 088	4 211
Nights spent by non-residents	10 676	11 891	12 313
of which: EU share (%)	86.1	81.6	81.6

Resident and non-resident shares of total nights spent in hotels and similar establishments - 2000

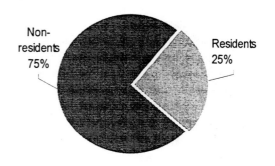

Arrivals at the borders ('000)

	1998	1999	2000
Visitors	3 267	4 088	4 293
Tourists	3 095	3 817	4 113

Balance of Payments - Travel (Mio EURO)

	1998	1999	2000
Credits	1 557	1 830	2 209
Debits	378	424	466
Balance	1 179	1 405	1 743

Travel item in the Balance of Payments (Mio EURO)

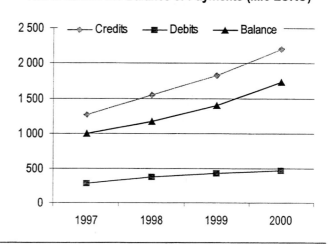

PALESTINE

Key statistics - 2000

Population	3 150 000
Surface area	6 022 km²
Population density (inhabitants/km²)	523.1
Increase in GDP	:
Exchange rate 1 EURO = US$	0.921937
Increase of consumer price index	2.8 %
Increase of hotels, cafés and restaurants consumer price index	:

Recent trends

The rise in the number of accommodation establishments and bed-places has kept in pace with growth in the tourism sector in Palestine. In 2000 there were 15 more establishments and 1,298 bed-places than in 1999 (+ 16%).

The total number of nights spent in hotels and similar establishments during 2000 increased by 13.1% compared to 1999, indicating a much lower annual growth rate than those of the previous few years. Non-resident nights increased by 16.9% and residents nights by 10.8%. Nights spent by EU tourists increased by 14.9%, accounting for 62% of foreign tourist nights. Tourists from the United States and Canada formed 11% of total non-resident nights in 2000.

Tourism is considered to be an important sector for the economic development of Palestine. In terms of foreign trade international travel receipts account for a very large share of services receipts, representing 79.2% in 1999. In terms of current account receipts, travel receipts represented 14.5% in 1999. International travel receipts rose by 13.5% compared to 1998, and the travel surplus rose by 24.9%.

The hotel and catering sector employed 8,782 persons in 1999, increasing by 8.4% compared to 1998.

Total nights spent in hotels and similar establishments ('000)

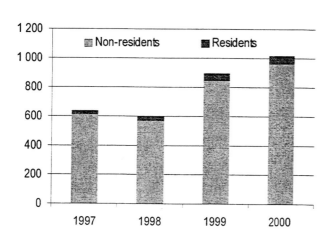

Key figures on tourism

Hotels and similar establishments

	1999	2000
Number of establishments	91	106
Number of bed-places	8 102	9 400
Average net rate of utilisation (%)	30.3	29.6

Nights spent in hotels and similar establishments (000s)

	1998	1999	2000
Total nights spent	601	896	1 017
Nights spent by residents	36	47	53
Nights spent by non-residents	565	848	964
of which: EU share (%)	54.9	57.7	62.1

Resident and non-resident shares of total nights spent in hotels and similar establishments - 2000

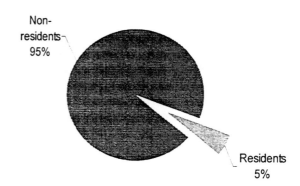

Balance of Payments - Travel (Mio EURO)

	1998	1999	2000
Credits	309	350	:
Debits	242	267	:
Balance	67	83	:

Travel item in the Balance of Payments (Mio EURO)

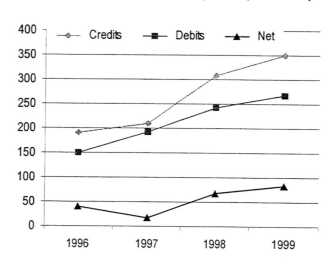

SYRIA

Key statistics - 2000

Population	16 320 000
Surface area	185 180 km²
Population density (inhabitants/km²)	88.1
Increase in GDP*	-1.8%
Exchange rate 1 EURO =* SYP	52.01
Increase of consumer price index	-0.9%
Increase of hotels, cafés and restaurants consumer price index	:

*1999

Recent trends

In 1999 the number of hotels and similar establishments grew by 8% (+36) compared to the previous year, and bed-places rose by 6% (+1,884).

In 1999 total nights spent in hotels and similar establishments remained stable (+0.6%) compared to 1998, amounting to nearly 3 million. The 2% decrease in nights spent by residents was compensated for by a 2% increase in the number of non-resident nights. Guests from the EU represented nearly 27% of non-resident nights in 1999; Europe as a whole represented 37%.

Total arrivals at the borders of visitors increased by 8.8% in 1999 compared to 1998. The overriding majority of visitors come from Arab countries, accounting for 74% of total arrivals in 1999. EU visitors only represented 5%. The number of tourists (overnight visitors) represents 34% of total visitor arrivals. Tourist arrivals increased by 3% in 1999. EU tourists represented 15% of total tourist arrivals and compared to 1998 their number grew by 17%.

International travel receipts increased by 21% in 2000 compared to 1999. Expenditures of Syrians travelling abroad also rose at a similar pace. In 2000 international travel receipts accounted for 14% of Syria's total current account foreign trade earnings and 64% of international Services receipts. Employment in the hotel and catering sector amounted to 36,900 employees in 1999.

Total nights spent in hotels and similar establishments ('000)

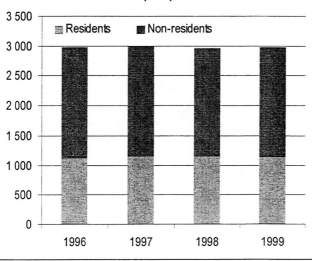

Key figures on tourism

Hotels and similar establishments

	1999	2000
Number of establishments	474	:
Number of bed-places	33 412	:
Average net rate of utilisation (%)	:	:

Nights spent in hotels and similar establishments (000s)

	1998	1999	2000
Total nights spent	2 962	2 978	:
Nights spent by residents	1 158	1 133	:
Nights spent by non-residents	1 804	1 845	:
of which: EU share (%)	23.0	26.6	:

Resident and non-resident shares of total nights spent in hotels and similar establishments – 1999

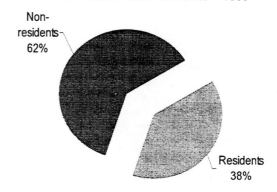

Arrivals at the borders ('000)

	1998	1999	2000
Visitors	2 464	2 682	:
Tourists	890	916	:

Balance of Payments - Travel (Mio EURO)

	1998	1999	2000
Credits	1 061	967	1 174
Debits	517	592	726
Balance	544	375	448

Travel item in the Balance of Payments (Mio EURO)

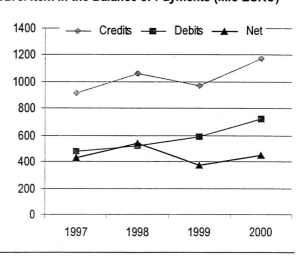

TUNISIA

Key statistics - 2000

Population [1]	9 457 000
Surface area	163 610 km²
Population density (inhabitants/km²)	57.8
Increase in GDP*	5.0%
Exchange rate 1 EURO = TND	1.2631
Increase of consumer price index	2.9%
Increase of hotels, cafés and restaurants consumer price index	:

* provisional data. [1] 1999 data

Recent trends

In 2000 there were 14 more hotels and similar establishments (+ 1.9%) amounting to 5,498 more bed-places (+2.9%) than in 1999.

In 2000 the total number of nights spent in hotels and similar establishments remained stable (+0.3%) compared to the previous year. Nights spent by non-residents represent 94% of total nights. Total arrivals at the borders of foreign visitors reached new heights in 2000, amounting to over 5 million, compared to 4.8 million in 1999. In 2000 total arrivals increased by 4.6%. The share of foreign visitor arrivals of EU citizens represented 64% in 2000, increasing in number by 5.6% over the previous year. The main EU generating markets are Germany, France and Italy.

Tourism is an important sector of the Tunisian economy. As international arrivals have been increasing, so have Tunisia's tourism foreign trade receipts. In 2000 travel receipts grew by 7.2% compared to 1999, and the travel surplus by 5.5%. Whereas, Tunisia's overall foreign trade balance is negative, it enjoys a surplus in its travel account. Travel receipts accounted for 18% of total foreign trade earnings and 61% of total receipts in services in 1999. Direct employment in the tourism industry accounted for 73, 846 jobs in 1998.

Total nights spent in hotels and similar establishments ('000)

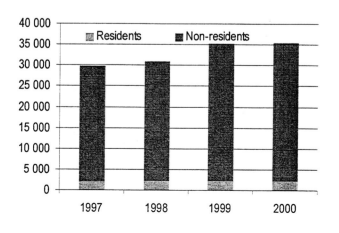

Key figures on tourism

Hotels and similar establishments

	1999	2000
Number of establishments	722	736
Number of bed-places	191 955	197 453
Average net rate of utilisation (%)	56.5	55.8

Nights spent in hotels and similar establishments (000s)

	1998	1999	2000
Total nights spent	30 982	35 320	35 424
Nights spent by residents	2 194	2 169	2 255
Nights spent by non-residents	28 788	33 151	33 168
of which: EU share (%)	77.4	86.3	86.8

Resident and non-resident shares of total nights spent in hotels and similar establishments – 2000

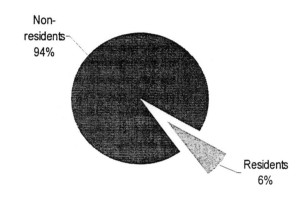

Non-residents 94%

Residents 6%

Arrivals at the borders ('000)

	1998	1999	2000
Visitors	5 218	5 915	:
Foreign visitors	4 718	4 832	5 058

Balance of Payments - Travel (Mio EURO)

	1998	1999	2000
Credits	1 477	1 708	1 831
Debits	209	224	266
Balance	1 268	1 485	1 566

Travel item in the Balance of Payments (Mio EURO)

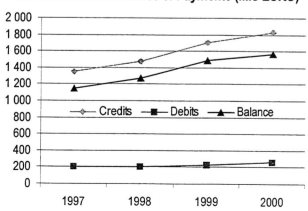

TURKEY

Key statistics - 2000

Population	67 377 000
Surface area	769 604 km²
Population density (inhabitants/km²)	87.5
Increase in GDP	7.2%
Exchange rate 1 EURO = TRL	574816.0
Increase of consumer price index	54.9%
Increase of hotels, cafés and restaurants consumer price index	:

Recent trends

In 2000 there were 48 less hotels and similar establishments (-2.7%) than in 1999, but capacity in terms of bed-places grew by 5.1%.

Total nights spent in hotels and similar establishments in 2000 increased by 17.5%, after a drop of 29% in 1999. This momentary slump was due to the 45% decrease in non-resident nights. Resident nights, on the other hand, continued the gradual upward trend of the previous years, albeit at a lesser rate (1.4% in 2000, 5.3 % in 1999).

After the severe slump in 1999, international visitor arrivals attained new heights in 2000 with over 10.4 million. Arrivals of EU visitors represented 53% of total visitor arrivals. Tourists account for 92% of all visitor arrivals to Turkey. Tourist arrivals amounted to over 9.5 million.

Tourism plays an important part in the Turkish economy. An indication of its contribution to employment are the 169,455 employees in the Ministry of Tourism licensed establishments (accommodation, restaurants, travel agencies and yacht crews) in 1998. In terms of foreign trade earnings, travel receipts represent 10% of Turkey's current account receipts in 1999 and 32% of services receipts. Turkey enjoys a positive tourism foreign trade balance, which fell substantially in 1999 due to the drop in receipts.

Total nights spent in hotels and similar establishments (000')

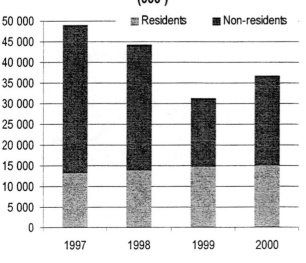

Key figures on tourism

Hotels and similar establishments

	1999	2000
Number of establishments	1 781	1 733
Number of bed-places	258 578	271 689
Average net rate of utilisation (%)	37.1	36.8

Nights spent in hotels and similar establishments (000s)

	1998	1999	2000
Total nights spent	44 253	31 342	36 817
Nights spent by residents	13 966	14 701	14 913
Nights spent by non-residents	30 287	16 641	21 904
of which: EU share (%)	68.4	53.1	59.5

Resident and non-resident shares of total nights spent in hotels and similar establishments - 2000

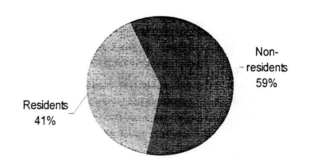

Arrivals at the borders ('000)

	1998	1999	2000
Visitors	9 431	7 487	10 428
Tourists	8 638	6 893	9 586

Balance of Payments - Travel (Mio EURO)

	1998	1999	2000
Credits	6 402	4 882	8 283
Debits	1 565	1 380	1 856
Balance	4 837	3 502	6 427

Travel item in the Balance of Payments (Mio EURO)

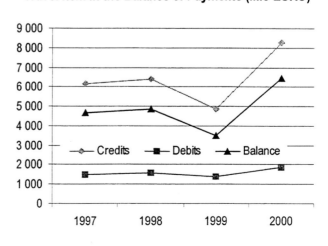

Technical Note

For the EU and EFTA countries, the data used in this publication come from Eurostat's information system "TOUR" in New Cronos (Theme 4).

The data collection on tourism at European level is based on Council Directive 95/57/EC, adopted 23 November 1995. The Directive provides a basic set of variables on tourism supply and demand, for which European Union member states are collecting data on a regular basis.

For the Central European and Mediterranean countries, the data used in this publication are principally based on information provided by the National Statistical Offices and/or National Tourism Authorities. Monetary figures are presented in Euro calculated according to the respective average annual exchange rates. In some cases the conversion into Euro has been made using the US$ exchange rate. Due to differences in data collection methods, definitions and other methodological approaches used by these countries, the data are not harmonised and thus not comparable. The geographical grouping of "Europe" refers generally to that used by the World Tourism Organisation.

The terminology specific to tourism used in this publication is fully in line with the definitions developed by Eurostat in the Community Methodology on Tourism Statistics.

Other Eurostat data sources used in the publication are Balance of Payments, Labour Force Surveys, Population, GDP(for European, Central European and EFTA countries: GDP at market prices, and for Mediterranean countries: GDP in volume), Euro Exchange Rate, Increase of Consumer Price Index (available in Eurostat's reference data base New Cronos). Population figures refer to 1 Jan 2000.

: = not available

Currency: Millions of EURO (from 1.1.1999) – Millions of ECU (up to 31.12.1998)

EU share of nights spent by non-residents: Share of non-resident tourists originating from other EU countries in relation to the world total.

Terms and definitions:

TOURISM is the activities of persons travelling to and staying in places *outside their usual environment* for not more than one consecutive year for leisure, business and other purposes.

Domestic tourism[1] comprises the activities of residents of a given area travelling only within that area, but outside their usual environment;

Inbound tourism as comprises the activities of non-residents travelling in a given area that is outside their usual environment;

Outbound tourism comprises the activities of residents of a given area travelling to and staying in places outside that area (and outside their usual environment).

---

[1] The term "Domestic" in the tourism context differs from its use in the System of National Accounts. In the national accounts context it refers to activities and expenditures of both residents and non- residents travelling within the given area, which in tourism terms is domestic and inbound tourism.

VISITORS: persons travelling to a place other than that of his/her usual environment for less than twelve consecutive months and whose main purpose of travel is other than the exercise of an activity remunerated from within the place visited.

TOURISTS: overnight visitors

INTERNATIONAL TOURISTS: international visitors who stay at least one night in collective or private accommodation in the country visited.

TOURIST ACCOMMODATION is any facility that regularly or occasionally provides overnight accommodation for visitors.

COLLECTIVE TOURIST ACCOMMODATION ESTABLISHMENTS: Establishments which provide overnight lodging for the traveller in a room or some other unit. The number of places it provides must be greater than a specified minimum amount for groups of person exceeding a single family unit and all the places in the establishments must come under a common commercial-type management, even if it is non-profit making.

HOTELS AND SIMILAR ESTABLISHMENTS are collective accommodation establishments typified as being arranged in rooms, in numbers exceeding a specified minimum, and as providing certain services including room services and daily bed-making and cleaning of the sanitary facilities.

>HOTELS: comprise hotels, apartment hotels, motels, roadside inns, beach hotels, residential clubs and similar establishments providing hotel services including more than daily bed-making and cleaning of the room and sanitary facilities.
>SIMILAR ESTABLISHMENTS: comprise rooming and boarding houses, tourist residence and similar accommodation arranged in rooms and providing limited hotel services including daily bed-making and cleaning of the room and sanitary facilities. This group also includes guesthouses, Bed & Breakfast and farmhouse accommodation.

OTHER COLLECTIVE ESTABLISHMENTS: are any establishment, intended for tourists, which may be non-profit making, coming under a common management, providing minimum common services (not including daily bed-making) and not necessarily being arranged in rooms but perhaps in dwelling-type units, campsites or collective dormitories. These can be subdivided as follows:

>HOLIDAY DWELLINGS: include collective facilities under common management, such as clusters of houses or bungalows arranged as dwelling-type accommodation and providing limited hotel services (not including daily bed-making and cleaning).
>TOURIST CAMPSITES: consists of collective facilities in enclosed areas for tents, caravans, trailers and mobile homes. All come under common management and provide some tourist services (shop, information, and recreational activities).
>OTHER COLLECTIVE ESTABLISHMENTS N.E.C.: comprise youth hostels, tourist dormitories, group accommodation, holiday homes for the elderly, holiday accommodation for employees and workers' hotels, halls of residence for students and school dormitories, and other similar facilities that come under common management, have a social interest and are often subsidised.

ESTABLISHMENTS: the local unit is an enterprise or part thereof situated in a geographically identified place. At or from this place economic activity is carried out for which - save for certain exceptions - one or more persons work (even if only part-time) for one and the same enterprise.

BED-PLACES: The number of bed-places in an establishment or dwelling is determined by the number of persons who can stay overnight in the beds set up in the establishment (dwelling), ignoring any extra beds that may be set up by customer request. The term bed-place applies to a single bed, double bed being counted as two bed-places. The unit serves to measure the capacity of any type of accommodation. A bed-place is also a place on a pitch or in a boat on a mooring to accommodate one person. One camping pitch should equal four bed-places if the actual number of bed-places is not known.

NIGHTS SPENT BY RESIDENTS AND NON-RESIDENTS: a night spent (or overnight stay) is each night that a guest actually spends (sleeps or stays) or is registered (his/her physical presence there being unnecessary) in a collective accommodation establishment or in private tourism accommodation.

NET USE OF BEDPLACES: the net occupancy rate of bed-places in one month is obtained by dividing total overnight stays by the product of the bed-places on offer and the number of days when the bed-places are actually available for use (net of seasonal closures and other temporary closures for decoration, by police order, etc.) for the same group of establishments, multiplying the quotient by 100 to express the result as a percentage.

Balance of Payments data are in line with the definitions in the Balance of Payments Manual by the International Monetary Fund. The **"Balance of Payments"** is defined as the record of a countries international transactions with the rest of the world (or, in other words, transactions of its residents with non-residents). Data in this publication mainly focus on transactions concerning "Travel". *"Travel"* covers goods and services acquired from an economy by non-resident travellers during their stay on the territory of that economy and for their own use.

European Commission

Tourism — Europe, Central European countries, Mediterranean countries — Key figures 1999–2000

Luxembourg: Office for Official Publications of the European Communities

2001 — 48 p. — 21 x 29.7 cm

Theme 4: Industry, trade and services
Collection: Detailed tables

ISBN 92-894-2058-8

Price (excluding VAT) in Luxembourg: EUR 16

.... Eurostat Data Shops

BELGIQUE/BELGIË

Eurostat Data Shop
Bruxelles/Brussel
Planistat Belgique
Rue du Commerce 124
Handelsstraat 124
B-1000 Bruxelles/Brussel
Tél. (32-2) 234 67 50
Fax (32-2) 234 67 51
E-mail: datashop@planistat.be
URL: http://www.datashop.org/

DANMARK

DANMARKS STATISTIK
Bibliotek og Information
Eurostat Data Shop
Sejrøgade 11
DK-2100 København Ø
Tlf. (45) 39 17 30 30
Fax (45) 39 17 30 03
E-mail: bib@dst.dk
Internet:
http://www.dst.dk/bibliotek

DEUTSCHLAND

Statistisches Bundesamt
Eurostat Data Shop Berlin
Otto-Braun-Straße 70-72
(Eingang: Karl-Marx-Allee)
D-10178 Berlin
Tel. (49) 1888-644 94 27/28
Fax (49) 1888-644 94 30
E-Mail: datashop@destatis.de
URL:
http://www.eu-datashop.de/

ESPAÑA

INE
Eurostat Data Shop
Paseo de la Castellana, 183
Oficina 009
Entrada por Estébanez
Calderón
E-28046 Madrid
Tel. (34) 91 583 91 67
Fax (34) 91 579 71 20
E-mail:
datashop.eurostat@ine.es
URL: http://www.datashop.org/
Member of the MIDAS Net

FRANCE

INSEE Info service
Eurostat Data Shop
195, rue de Bercy
Tour Gamma A
F-75582 Paris Cedex 12
Tél. (33) 1 53 17 88 44
Fax (33) 1 53 17 88 22
E-mail: datashop@insee.fr
Member of the MIDAS Net

ITALIA - ROMA

ISTAT
Centro di informazione
statistica — Sede di Roma
Eurostat Data Shop
Via Cesare Balbo, 11a
I-00184 Roma
Tel. (39) 06 46 73 31 02/06
Fax (39) 06 46 73 31 01/07
E-mail: dipdiff@istat.it
Member of the MIDAS Net

ITALIA - MILANO

ISTAT
Ufficio regionale per la
Lombardia
Eurostat Data Shop
Via Fieno, 3
I-20123 Milano
Tel. (39) 02 80 61 32 460
Fax (39) 02 80 61 32 304
E-mail: mileuro@tin.it
Member of the MIDAS Net

LUXEMBOURG

Eurostat Data Shop
Luxembourg
BP 453
L-2014 Luxembourg
4, rue Alphonse Weicker
L-2721 Luxembourg
Tél. (352) 43 35-2251
Fax (352) 43 35-22221
E-mail:
dslux@eurostat.datashop.lu
URL: http://www.datashop.org/
Member of the MIDAS Net

NEDERLAND

STATISTICS NETHERLANDS
Eurostat Data Shop —
Voorburg
Postbus 4000
2270 JM Voorburg
Nederland
Tel. (31-70) 337 49 00
Fax (31-70) 337 59 84
E-mail: datashop@cbs.nl

PORTUGAL

Eurostat Data Shop Lisboa
INE/Serviço de Difusão
Av. António José de Almeida, 2
P-1000-043 Lisboa
Tel. (351) 21 842 61 00
Fax (351) 21 842 63 64
E-mail: data.shop@ine.pt

SUOMI/FINLAND

STATISTICS FINLAND
Eurostat DataShop Helsinki
Tilastokirjasto
PL 2B
FIN-00022 Tilastokeskus
Työpajakatu 13 B, 2. Kerros,
Helsinki
P. (358-9) 17 34 22 21
F. (358-9) 17 34 22 79
Sähköposti: datashop@stat.fi
URL:
http://tilastokeskus.fi/tk/kk/
datashop/

SVERIGE

STATISTICS SWEDEN
Information service
Eurostat Data Shop
Karlavägen 100
Box 24 300
S-104 51 Stockholm
Tfn (46-8) 50 69 48 01
Fax (46-8) 50 69 48 99
E-post: infoservice@scb.se
Internet:
http://www.scb.se/info/
datashop/eudatashop.asp

UNITED KINGDOM

Eurostat Data Shop
Enquiries & advice and
publications
Office for National Statistics
Customers & Electronic
Services Unit B1/05
1 Drummond Gate
London SW1V 2QQ
United Kingdom
Tel. (44-20) 75 33 56 76
Fax (44-1633) 81 27 62
E-mail:
eurostat.datashop@ons.gov.uk
Member of the MIDAS Net

Eurostat Data Shop
Electronic Data Extractions,
enquiries & advice r.cade
1L Mountjoy Research Centre
University of Durham
Durham DH1 3SW
United Kingdom
Tel. (44-191) 374 73 50
Fax (44-191) 384 49 71
E-mail: r-cade@dur.ac.uk
Internet:
http://www-rcade.dur.ac.uk

NORWAY

Statistics Norway
Library and Information Centre
Eurostat Data Shop
Kongens gate 6
Boks 8131 Dep.
N-0033 Oslo
Tel. (47) 21 09 46 42/43
Fax (47) 21 09 45 04
E-mail: Datashop@ssb.no

SCHWEIZ/SUISSE/SVIZZERA

Statistisches Amt des Kantons
Zürich
Eurostat Data Shop
Bleicherweg 5
CH-8090 Zürich
Tel. (41-1) 225 12 12
Fax (41-1) 225 12 99
E-mail:
datashop@statistik.zh.ch
Internet:
http://www.zh.ch/statistik

USA

HAVER ANALYTICS
Eurostat Data Shop
60 East 42nd Street
Suite 3310
New York, NY 10165
Tel. (1-212) 986 93 00
Fax (1-212) 986 69 81
E-mail: eurodata@haver.com

EUROSTAT HOME PAGE
www.europa.eu.int/comm/eurostat/

MEDIA SUPPORT
EUROSTAT
(only for professional journalists)
Postal address:
Jean Monnet building
L-2920 Luxembourg
Office: BECH A3/48 —
5, rue Alphonse Weicker
L-2721 Luxembourg
Tel. (352) 43 01-33408
Fax (352) 43 01-32649
E-mail:
Eurostat-mediasupport@cec.eu.int